We Remember

THE

HOME
GUARD

We Remember

THE

HOME
GUARD

FRANK & JOAN SHAW

EBURY
PRESS

1 3 5 7 9 10 8 6 4 2

Published in 2012 by Ebury Press, an imprint of
Ebury Publishing
A Random House Group company
First published in the UK by Frank Shaw and Joan Shaw in 1990

Collection © Frank Shaw and Joan Shaw 1990, 2012

Frank Shaw and Joan Shaw have asserted their right to be
identified as the authors of this Work in accordance with the
Copyright, Designs and Patents Act 1988

The Random House Group Limited Reg. No. 954009

Addresses for companies within the Random House Group can
be found at www.randomhouse.co.uk

A CIP catalogue record for this book is available from
the British Library

The Random House Group Limited supports The Forest
Stewardship Council (FSC®), the leading international forest
certification organisation. Our books carrying the FSC label are
printed on FSC® certified paper. FSC is the only forest certification
scheme endorsed by the leading environmental organisations,
including Greenpeace. Our paper procurement policy can be found
at www.randomhouse.co.uk/environment

Printed and bound by CPI Group (UK) Ltd, Croydon, CR0 4YY

ISBN 9780091941536

To buy books by your favourite authors and register for offers
visit www.randomhouse.co.uk

Contents

Foreword

A little over forty years ago I got a nice TV job of seven episodes of something called *Dad's Army* that would last me through the summer of 1968. Little did I know that it would still, happily, be with me all these years later.

I knew a little about the Home Guard already. My father had been a policeman during the war in the industrial Midlands. He was the station sergeant and in their local set up was the officer who liaised between the Home Guard units and the Army Bomb Disposal Units. He had a few tales to tell about it all but not enough to prevent me from doing the first job of any actor, my own research, when *Dad's Army* arrived.

Libraries and the Imperial War Museum were quite informative, providing many facts and figures, and dry dusty statistics often with the jingoistic tone of the newsreels of the time. In reality there was nothing jingoistic about the thousands of men (and in many places women) who volunteered to become an army on the home front; an army in their non-working hours, their normally sleeping hours, in order to guard factories and infrastructure, to firewatch and to scan the night-time skies, and to supplement and bolster the full-time 'real' army.

They may not have known it when they volunteered, but I am totally confident that had the horror of the threat of invasion become reality they would have become just as 'real' as the full-timers and stood up to be counted, and been counted without hesitation or question.

Over the ten years of making *Dad's Army* (more than twice the life of the Home Guard itself) I flatter myself that we entertained a large number of people and we were led to believe that these millions did in fact include many veterans of the Home Guard. Its co-writer and producer David Croft proudly claimed that he received only one letter of violent complaint from the public and that was about the depiction of a slightly fey vicar. We never for one moment were, or thought we might be, disrespectful of the members of the Home Guard. Nor did we ever think that we were presenting a historical portrait of it either. It was a comedy programme set in a fictional town populated by imaginary characters for whom we all had a great affection and, I assure you, an enormous respect for the reality that they were set in.

There is no shortage of contemporary or retrospective histories of the services armed or secret. Even the home front is chronicled. The Mass Observation project – started in 1937 after the abdication of Edward VIII

– continued through the war and after, and it provides an amazing social history of the domestic war, but where is the everyday story of the Home Guard?

One of the happy side-effects of *Dad's Army* was the growth of interest in the ordinary men and women, and youths who responded to Anthony Eden's broadcast and joined the Local Defence Volunteers.

Frank and Joan Shaw began their project 23 years ago when their daughter set out on a school project about the Second World War.

They engaged the help of over 700 local newspapers to request the memories of the men who went out on parade and patrol night after night following their normal day's work. The result is this extraordinary collection of often endearing, inspiring and sometimes amazing stories from men in their teens to their seventies, which provides a slightly wider resource than the regulars.

It is no fusty history but a collection of memories in the men's own words; a collection to dip into for five minutes or an hour; to work through chronologically or to wander about within in whatever direction may take your fancy. You will approach these people like old friends finding out what made them tick, what made them hurt, what made them laugh or cry. They will also tell you stories that are far more outrageous than anything used in *Dad's Army*.

I am proud to have been in *Dad's Army*; I am proud

to have been asked to write a forward to this collection; and I am proud to have known a few men like those you will meet in the following pages.

Ian Lavender
2012

Introduction

With the fall of Dunkirk on 5 June 1940, the German Armies turned south and poured across France, entering Paris on 14 June. Flushed with victory and confidence, provided with overwhelming air support and led by armoured formations that shattered the French defences, it was all over in a matter of days.

On 22 June 1940 France surrendered. Great Britain now stood alone.

It was a daunting prospect. The BEF – British Expeditionary Force – had been saved but had lost almost all its equipment. Now everything would depend on the Royal Navy and the Royal Air Force to prevent an invasion. But if they failed...?

The Local Defence Volunteers, LDV, had been formed on 14 May 1940 as the Government began to realise what could happen. They came from all walks of life. Those already in full-time work: miners, farmworkers, dockers, bus drivers, clerks and fishermen; those too young to join up; the elderly and retired and those too old for the Armed Forces; men in 'reserved occupations', who could not be 'called up' because of the importance of their work. Everyone not serving in the Armed Forces became involved, either as members of the LDV or in some support capacity.

Their weapons and ammunition were negligible. Not least because even the Regular Army was without its basic equipment. But everything from pitchforks to Boer War rifles was used. The message was simple: if you owned it and it could be used as an offensive weapon, then it was accepted.

It has been suggested that it was the uniform that really brought out the hidden talents of this 'Citizens Army', and there is a great deal of truth in this. Would the LDV, or Home Guard, have functioned at all if it had consisted of men simply in civilian clothes with no common identification? We doubt it. But when given a uniform or even an armband they became part of an organisation, and that created a feeling of 'belonging' and responsibility to the organisation. In that situation you feel 'needed'. You are identified. People depend on you. You don't want to let them down.

But there is another factor that we believe has not been considered, and that is the change of name. On 28 July 1940, two months after the LDV was set up, Winston Churchill showed his genius and grasp of the British character when he changed the name from 'Local Defence Volunteers' to 'Home Guard'. Consider the name 'Local Defence Volunteers'. It is imprecise

('Local'), negative ('Defence') and sounds amateurish ('Volunteers'). The new name is the opposite. It is precise ('Home') and both positive and professional ('Guard').

By that simple change of name Churchill immediately sent out in our darkest hour a message of both responsibility and hope to every citizen in Great Britain. The Army had been saved. The Royal Navy and the Royal Air Force were intact. Now every citizen was involved as well through this new national organisation 'The Home Guard'.

Churchill was at his stirring best when he said, in the summer of 1940:

The whole of the warring nations are engaged, not only soldiers but the entire population, men, women and children. The fronts are everywhere. The trenches are dug in the towns and streets. Every village is fortified. Every road is barred. The front lines run through the factories. The workmen are soldiers with different weapons – but the same courage.

With these words ringing in their ears, millions both joined and supported the Home Guard. At first many were armed with nothing more lethal than a pickaxe, but they drilled, practised, exercised and learnt.

*

Members of the Home Guard were the great unpaid, unwashed, unfed and part-time, part-worn, sockless, shirtless, breathless army, who were supposed in their respective duties to know how to become crack shots with a rifle, desperate bayonet fighters, all-in wrestlers, expert throwers of hand grenades, and long-distance runners.

They were expected to know the length and weight of a rifle and all its independent component parts, also the weight and characteristics of all grenades and bombs. They were supposed to be expert machine gunners, scientific engineers, and fully qualified Bren gunners. There were, of course, numerous other weapons of war with which they were expected to be fully conversant, but as only 3 million other men knew about them, this was considered secret.

Apart from this they were supposed to know the exact positions of local post and telegraph offices, railway stations, police stations, routes to neighbouring towns and villages, telephone systems and positions of locally available instruments; a knowledge of local hostels, treatment of foot and mouth disease, and general guidance to waifs and strays was also considered helpful.

A Home Guard was expected at all times and under all conditions to exercise tact when answering the commanding officer, and also factious labourers who complained of fairy footsteps in the early morning. He was expected to emulate the contortions of Houdini in arranging kit, study the artifices of the rubber man, and be fully proficient in the Indian rope trick.

They were of course expected to know the history of their section, the names of their Platoon and Company Commanders, and (never having seen him) be able to recognise their Colonel instantly on sight. Although they had never even heard of him, they were expected to know the name of their Zone Commander.

They had to know the address, location and nearest route to Company Battalion, and Zone Headquarters (which were probably changing overnight without their knowledge) and had to be expert in fieldcraft, street fighting, lead swinging, map reading, dart throwing, and defence in depth.

They had to know how to deal with paratroops, catty wives, telephones, lice, stooges and landlords; how to move unseen and unheard through the back door of the local, and how to camouflage their positions from air observation and how to use natural cover when the rent man called.

They had to be adept at crawling on underfed tummies through ploughed fields and undergrowth, and how, in short, to convert themselves from clerk, shopkeeper or mechanic who wouldn't hurt a fly in the daytime into a bloody assassin with a dagger at night.

How to detect and deal with all types of gases, both known and unknown, fully understand decontamination, salvation, abomination, damnation, and all the other blasted nationalities were also requirements of the Home Guard.

Most certainly they had to know how to destroy tanks, battle cruisers and how to erect roadblocks. Above all else they had to know how to provide themselves with iron rations without means, without points, and without any bloody hope! They had to show restraint when returning from an eight-hour exercise to find the local dodgers had swiped all the beer, or the landlords had spragged the barrels.

Finally, all Home Guards had to attend first-aid lectures, to acquire a thorough knowledge of splints, tumours, pimples and pollution, smells, stinks and change of life, and in conclusion they were advised to qualify in midwifery and so prepare for any grave emergency which may have arisen.

Having done all this they were then expected to earn their living (if time permitted) but above all they had to mount guard each week, for which they were paid 18 pence to be spent on such luxuries as loose living and debauchery.

By 'stand down' in 1944 they had acquired a formidable array of weaponry and were trained to professional standards.

As it happened, they were not called upon to take on the might and power of the German army and its Panzers. But if this island of ours had been invaded, there is little doubt that the Home Guard would have acquitted itself with the greatest credit and bravery. Almost certainly it would ultimately have failed to prevent a total military occupation, but that would not have been for lack of effort. Just lack of equipment.

But there is this. If there had been such a military occupation by the Nazis, there is no doubt that very many Home Guards, right across the country, would have formed guerilla groups and carried out guerilla warfare almost indefinitely at enormous cost to the German forces.

Many of the recollections in this book refer to humorous incidents. We now know that they were not ultimately required to fight and so, recognising that they were not 'Regulars', many of these personal recollections now dwell on the 'amateurish' nature of the Home Guard and the laughs and mistakes. That is understandable because basically they were amateurs, and the ever-popular TV series *Dad's Army* has concentrated on that aspect.

But do not forget that these 'amateurs', in less than four years, did achieve a real professional, military competence. And with all due respect to the Regular Army, they did it not as a full-time occupation but as very much a part-time one, which was often both dangerous and arduous.

Many also had full-time jobs, often little sleep, and they were initially in an organisation that was totally new to them. Others were elderly and retired and did not have these problems – but nevertheless they were prepared to sacrifice what should have been their 'last, peaceful years' to face a fearful foe.

So when you read these recollections, enjoy the laughs and the human weaknesses that are revealed. But do not forget the modesty that lies behind this self-effacement, and that these were the same men who were prepared to fight and die for their country as part of a Citizens Army if called upon to do so.

All these years later we can laugh with them. But laugh *with* them and not *at* them, because if there had been an invasion in 1940 we have no doubt we would have had cause to be proud of them.

Frank and Joan Shaw

AUTHORS' NOTE

The addresses at the end of each entry refer to the location the letters were sent from, not necessarily where the letter writer lived during the war.

PART I

The LDV

'When you write any account of the Local Defence Volunteers (or Home Guard as it later became) you must realise the tremendous spirit and enthusiasm of those early volunteers. We were in fact civilians trying to learn the arts of war, and not much time to do it in… The spirit was such that many years later and after the war, one of my old Home Guard sergeants said to me just before he died, "There will never be the spirit in this country again that we had in those old days of the LDV."'

JOSEPH O'KEEFE, DUNSTON, GATESHEAD

Came the black year of 1940. Great Britain was fighting alone and had its back to the wall. From the bombed beaches of Dunkirk the outcast and ill-equipped British Expeditionary Force had been brought back safely to the shores of England by thousands of small craft under the protective guns of the Royal Navy. 'We shall fight on the beaches, in the hills and in the streets, we shall never surrender,' roared Winston Churchill. The man really meant it.

To defend Britain's shores from the threat of a German invasion a new army was being formed. Anybody from 16 to 70 was welcome. This new army was termed the Local Defence Volunteers.

I rushed to join it. I would have got in if I'd have only had one leg. I was accepted immediately and fitted out with a pair of wellingtons (a size too large), one steel helmet that nearly covered my shoulders, and a ground-sheet that could have been made for 'King Kong'. My kit was finally completed when the portly quartermaster sergeant handed me a brand-new cap badge of the West Yorkshire Regiment and one khaki armband sporting the legend LDV.

'Report to the drill hall tomorrow night son, seven o'clock sharp,' he said with a comradely wink. 'We'll soon have you ship-shape and ready for action.'

Not knowing the army procedure for addressing a quartermaster sergeant of the LDV, I gave him a wink back. That will do for starters I thought, skipping smartly through the door. Honest to God I still have a quiet chuckle to myself when I think of the way his waxed moustache curled up at the ends when I threw him the wink. For a 16-year-old defender of the King's Realm I still had a lot to learn.

At the drill hall one rifle was allocated to every ninth man. The rest of the men had to drill with long broom handles. My crowning glory came one Sunday evening when the squad was marched through the city centre to guard Bradford's Electricity Power Station. We made a brave sight as we marched through Forster Square. For this special occasion every man had been kitted out with a denim battledress and a Lee-Enfield rifle. With flowing groundsheets we left wheeled into Canal Road amidst thunderous applause from two old dears.

'They're off to fight the Germans,' said one to the other.

With steel helmet tilted to one side of my head so as not to spoil my waves, I marched along six foot tall. The icing on the cake came two hours later when the guard commander handed me five live rounds of ammunition.

'Let's hope no more than five of 'em land, Private Scully,' he crowed sarcastically, leading me to my guard posting.

The next two hours I spent scanning the night sky above Bradford's pylons for invading German paratroopers, and praying to God they would pick my territory for their invasion assault. Such is the ignorance of youth when playing at war. Even today I have violent shudders just thinking about it.

Eventually the LDV (cruelly termed by some as the Look, Duck and Vanish Brigade) was renamed the Home Guard, and was quickly transformed into a well equipped and highly efficient defence force consisting of over 2 million well trained men, but in its infancy...? Least said the better.

Bill Scully
BRADFORD, WEST YORKSHIRE

It all began after Dunkirk when we were threatened with invasion. Anthony Eden, the Foreign Secretary, appealed over the radio for civilian volunteers to help repel German troops that were expected to descend on us at any moment. The new force was to be called The Local Defence Volunteers or LDV for short. As in all aspects of life, nothing is sacred and it wasn't long before the comedians on the radio were dubbing us The Look, Duck and Vanishers. Very droll.

My part in all this commenced when my mother, a small, wiry, fierce character, called a family conference to decide who amongst us were going to join and answer the call to arms. My father, a First World War veteran who for years had been telling us how he had just been waiting to have a go at the Jerries again, remained strangely silent. My two elder

brothers protested that they would be called up soon anyway and as my younger brother was too young at the time, all the heads swung in my direction. So, one day after my eighteenth birthday, I became a member of the Kennington Company in what was called M Zone Local Defence Volunteers, South London.

We had, of course, no arms of any description. At first, in fact, they didn't really know what to do with us so they sent us out to check the Identity Cards of people travelling on buses. The only visible authority we had for this momentous task was an armband with LDV in bold black lettering. All went swimmingly at first but then we came across a young girl on the top deck of a bus who had no Identity Card. She had left it at home.

We gave her a stern rebuke and, of course, she burst into tears. Well we hadn't been warned about this and were at a loss what to do but we soon made up our minds what to do when all the men on the bus started to abuse us. We fled.

Shortly after this we were provided with a denim uniform and army boots, so at last we were beginning to feel like semi-soldiers. So many people soak up that silly programme called *Dad's Army* but in truth it should have been called *Kid's Army* for that is what it was. The majority of our company were youngsters like myself and my kid brother who was 15 at the time. We had a few old soldiers and naturally they became our officers and NCOs.

Fred Woolford
ROMFORD, ESSEX

The need to create such a force of civilian soldiers arose of course out of the dire situation in which this country found itself in the struggle against Fascism. The German Armed Forces seemed invincible. They had swept through the Low Countries after devastating Poland, occupied Norway, shattered France, and were expected to launch an assault against England within days. Church bells were silenced, to be rung again only if or when invading forces were approaching these shores. Our army, or that part of it that had been plucked from the beaches of Dunkirk, had to be reformed and re-equipped ready to meet the threatened onslaught. More than that, the whole nation had to mobilise as never before to fight for this nation's very survival.

There was a Civil Defence Force in existence, set up in the month before the outbreak of hostilities when war seemed inevitable. But a Home Guard wasn't part of that force. It was born of urgent necessity, a Citizens' Army to be used in what might be the United Kingdom's last-ditch effort. We were all, without doubt, 'in it'.

My 'call to arms' came when I was working at Birch Mills to where I had been directed after having failed my medical at Dover Street, Manchester. No service in the 'real' Armed Forces for me, so the advent of 'Dad's Army' gave me the chance to do my bit although it was to be another three years before I actually became a dad.

A Home Guard unit, of platoon strength I think, was duly formed. Its primary duty was to guard and defend a factory engaged in vital war work. How vital it was wasn't really known until the war was nearly over. Without doubt when we at last donned battledress it was to be ready to put our lives (plus cards and dominoes) on the line whenever Max Schmelling and his fellow German parachute troops might descend on Birch village.

Getting kitted out was quite an experience. An armband was our uniform, together with a brush handle. This was supposed to scare off the aforementioned sky troops of the Third Reich. However, came the day when a notice on the works noticeboard announced that some uniforms and a certain amount of equipment had arrived, and would be issued in time for the Invasion.

Battledress two sizes too big, trousers baggy and inches too long, ankle length greatcoats later to serve as bedspreads, forage caps that covered head, eyes and ears, boots that increased one's height by two inches and weight by more than a few pounds. Leather anklets, two ammunition pouches, a tin helmet, a groundsheet-cum-cape, a gas cape and haversack completed our issue. All we needed now was weaponry to make us ready to face the best, or the worst, that Hitler could send against us. Well, some weapons of war did arrive; one rifle (Canadian Ross) between three men. Charge hands had one each. A few bayonets and fewer still .303 bullets which had to be kept in the guard room at all times except when issued to lads on guard duty when the bullets were stuffed in greatcoat pockets to be fumbled for should there be an alert.

John Slawson
HEYWOOD, LANCASHIRE

I was only 16 years old when war was declared in 1939, therefore I did not get into the RAF until early 1942. In the meantime, the forming of the Local Defence Volunteers (later called the Home Guard) was announced [and] I joined the same day.

The majority of LDV members were ex-soldiers too old to join the Forces, but nonetheless enthusiastic. It was a constant source of amazement to me that no matter what the training consisted of and no matter where we went to on a Sunday morning, the Old Soldier in charge never failed to dismiss us at precisely one minute to opening time outside The Nag's Head pub.

The equipment we had at that time, or more accurately the lack of it, produced some ingenious ideas. One weapon consisted of a length of ordinary drainpipe, a six-foot brush handle, a penny balloon, a wooden bung with a hole in it, a small amount of powder, and a detonator that would be fired by a torch battery.

The idea was that the balloon would be primed with powder and detonator, and the detonator wire passed through the wooden bung to be attached to the battery. The bung would be pushed into the back of the drainpipe. The brush handle with an explosive charge attached to the front of it would be pushed into the drainpipe from the other end, but during practice the explosive would be replaced with a wooden block. The whole lot would then be buried at the side of the road on which enemy tanks were expected to come.

Came the day for testing this marvellous secret weapon. Arrangements had been made previously with the Regular Army that a row of tanks would travel down the road at a reasonable speed and nicely spaced out for us to fire at. I was hidden behind the hedge ready to throw the switch when my friend observing from a nearby tree gave the signal.

Then it happened. My friend waved. I threw the switch. The broom handle did as was expected, just shot out

into the road. However, it jammed the wooden block into the tank track causing the tank to swerve and skid through the hedge down the bank and almost turn over. Fantastic – a direct hit.

When the tank driver and his crew crawled out of the tank bruised and battered, from the looks they gave me I would have been well advised to do what I had been told to do in actual battle conditions. I did it. I made myself scarce as quickly as possible.

The officers analysing the situation afterwards agreed that the tank would have been destroyed, but myself and my friend would also probably have been killed by being too close to the explosion. Honour was satisfied all round.

With men and weapons like these could there ever have been any doubt as to the eventual outcome of the war?

Ernest Pearce
CLOWNE, CHESTERFIELD, DERBYSHIRE

When Sir Anthony Eden broadcast an appeal for volunteers in 1940 I was a student at Cambridge, living at home. Listening to him were my mother, 'C' – a research psychologist who lived with us as what was then called a PG, 'Permanent Guest', and myself.

Next morning I remember very clearly that 'C' and I went into the Police Station in Cambridge to sign on. The sergeant knew nothing of the Local Defence Volunteers, as they were first called. However, he took our names and recorded them on the back of an envelope. A week or two later, Grantchester LDV was formed under the captaincy of an ex-Indian army man. The sergeant was a First World War veteran and we numbered about 20 all told. Most of them were over 50.

Our weapons at that time were not impressive; a couple of shotguns, a pitchfork or two and later several pikes from the War Office. The latter might have impaled the occasional paratrooper but were hardly the kind of thing to give one confidence.

However, we found more satisfaction from the contribution of a local man who had hunted big game in Africa. As I remember it was a .405 elephant rifle, very heavy, with telescopic sights. I was designated its 'minder' on account of age and fitness. It had one drawback. The donor could find only 18 rounds of ammunition. The fact that the bullets were soft-nosed and against the Hague Convention did not worry us in the least, I remember, but the fact that we had so few did.

But it was important to test the weapon, so we all went to the local range and I fired one of our precious rounds. It proved to be deadly accurate at 500 yards.

About that time we also received our Lewis Gun. Evening sessions were spent taking it to pieces, learning how to fire, load magazines, unjam it when it jammed and clean it. My friend, 'C', found it difficult. He struggled not only with the bits of shiny metal that would not fit but also his gentle nature and his strong pacifist leanings. The theology professor was all fingers and thumbs. The classics professor, 'B', was a quick learner, however, and it was for that reason that he was entrusted with the next weapon that arrived, a Stokes Mortar. I was appointed his Number Two.

By this time the elephant rifle had been superseded by .303 rifles for everyone, bayonets, hand grenades and several anti-tank mines. In addition we spent time practising with our bottles of petrol fused with cotton wool called Molotov Cocktails.

Alan Lawrie
LUDLOW, SHROPSHIRE

My grandfather, in whose house we lived during the war, was a retired Gunner General, as were many of his friends and neighbours in Camberley and he soon became involved with the LDV and commanded the local unit, our house becoming the headquarters. Everybody was keen to join in and help defend the country. There were frequent exercises in our area and an enormous amount of planning would go into these. My bedroom was immediately above my grandfather's study and I could hear most of what was going on down below. There were lengthy phone calls  and my mother would act as Despatch Rider on her bicycle taking 'top secret' messages to other Commanders.

Mrs Jane Uren
TENTERDEN, KENT

I was a 23-year-old NCB Inspector of Haydon Road, Ashington, and joined the LDV within ten minutes of Anthony Eden's announcement. I served throughout the duration, mostly with the Stakeford Platoon. Son of a Grenadier Guardsman, I was educated at Guide Post Senior School and later worked at local collieries. Rumour has it that when a photograph of our belligerent group fell into the Fuhrer's hands, he abandoned the invasion plans forthwith and attacked the Soviet Union.

Tommy Wilkinson
ASHINGTON, NORTHUMBERLAND

I was my husband's second wife and he was 24 years older than I. One night we were listening to the 9 p.m. news and that was when we first heard of the Local Defence Volunteers as they were called at the beginning. My husband went straight to the telephone to volunteer and was straight away asked if he had any weapons. I remember that he replied that he had a German army rifle and a round of ammunition which he had taken from a German officer whom he had taken prisoner during the First World War in the German East Africa Campaign. He was told it would be very useful as they had no arms at present. A few days later he received his armband labelled LDV.

Hilda K. Burnet
HEMEL HEMPSTEAD, HERTFORDSHIRE

Although I enlisted the first day, I didn't get into training until I had complained to a customer saying it was several weeks since I had signed my form and I hadn't heard anything. She said she would have a word with her husband, and the result was the next day I got a word to report for parades at the local lecture hall and was issued with an armband with 'LDV' on it. Obviously I had spoken to a customer with power. The wife of someone of some rank in the Home Guard.

Later on we were issued with a denim uniform. You needed a neck like a horse to get a snug fit. You did not get your equipment all at one time. You would get your uniform, later you would get a belt, another time a haversack, then boots, and so it went on. I remember at one time everyone had to bring their own piece of string to use as a rifle sling. But through time we were all fully equipped and after a while we were looking a bit more military instead of a section of Fred Karno's Army.

Joseph O'Keefe
DUNSTON, GATESHEAD

I was a young man of 17 when I joined the Home Guard and after the fall of France and the return of our soldiers from Dunkirk things looked pretty serious. Certainly at that time we all thought that invasion was imminent. The LDV, as it was then, was established to protect important buildings in and around the town and to resist invasion.

I went along about a fortnight later and joined at the local barracks where we were formed into different companies. Mine was 'A' Company. We were given instructions about drills, and obeying orders from some old soldiers from the First World War, and we used to do guard duty at the main Post Office in the centre of town. When it was my turn I used to parade up and down outside the building until I was relieved by a colleague.

I have to confess that I thought that I was the bee's knees wearing a lovely blue sports jacket, and grey worsted flannels, with this very special armband on my sleeve with the words LDV on it.

In our area we had all been issued with all sorts of weapons. Many of them were farmers' shotguns, as that was virtually all that there was available at the time. I remember an amusing incident in the guardroom at the Post Office. One chap had his shotgun loaded and had accidentally caught the trigger, and he blew out half the windows of the Post Office building.

Another amusing incident was when we were on night exercises and expecting an attack from the Regular Army in the middle of a field on the outskirts of the town. It was about two o'clock in the morning, pitch black because of the blackout, and I was laid flat down with my rifle ready for any eventuality. Earlier we had fixed some tin cans on the wire fence of the field with bits of wire, and hopefully when the Regular soldiers climbed over the fence the tins would rattle and raise the alarm. At least that was the idea. Unfortunately it was a windy night and they were rattling all the time. As I lay there on my own I suddenly saw a dark shadow rather large coming towards me and I thought this is it.

In my mind I could already see four soldiers creeping up quietly towards me but I waited until they were almost on top of me when I suddenly leapt up and issued the challenge to them. The next thing I saw was a mighty shire horse galloping down past me and its hoof just missed my head by inches. We eventually got beaten by the army in that exercise, but I had a good laugh afterwards.

Robert A. Eland
SCARBOROUGH, YORKSHIRE

In July or August, 1940, Churchill prepared for the worst. Shrouded in secrecy, an underground army to surface when invasion took place was formed from the Home Guard. The organiser was a 44-year-old Major General Colin McGubbins, who set up a training establishment in a large country house, where that select band of the Home Guard learned to make Molotov Cocktails and other explosive devices before returning to their own areas to recruit 10 to 15 potential 'guerillas' to join their group. By the time this underground army was eventually dissolved, there were more than 1,000 bunkers scattered throughout Britain. In fact, when a false alarm was sounded on 7 September that the invasion was actually taking place, many of the male population of Scotland actually disappeared underground for a week, leaving other civilians wondering what had become of them.

Home Guard units at first had no NCO or officer ranks, but section leaders, platoon commanders, etc. Blue wool stripes on the shoulder straps indicated appointments, but as things got organised, armbands gave way to denim battledress uniform, worn over ordinary trousers,

shirt and pullover, etc. They in turn gave way to British Army battledress with black boots, leather gaiters (not webbing as supplied to the army), field service cap with badge of County Regiment, leather belt, greatcoat, haversack, gas mask and tin hat. Military ranks and badges with shoulder titles in yellow 'Home Guard', with county/battalion markings below. The rifles were .300s although the army had .303s. These were supplied from the USA together with bayonets. Each member of my platoon was issued with ten rounds, which they kept at home with their rifle and bayonet, usually under the bed.

Bob McGill
WEST HADDON, NORTHAMPTONSHIRE

When Anthony Eden made his appeal for Local Defence Volunteers in May 1940, I was 17 years old and an apprentice carpenter and joiner. With scores of other men, young and old, I went to Windsor Police Station where in a large crowded room we registered our names and addresses. A few days later I was asked to deliver armbands with the initials LDV printed on them, together with notices of the first meeting to be held at The Imperial Service College (a private school in the town) where we learned about the Lee-Enfield rifle.

After that we regularly paraded in the evenings to be taught the army drill movements, and I recall how proud we all were when the drills were carried out smartly. Naturally some of the older members were not as agile as we youngsters, and were perhaps like Corporal Jones in *Dad's Army*. There were, in fact, many like Captain Mainwaring, bumbling but fiercely patriotic.

Roy Elmer
WINDSOR, BERKSHIRE

S ome months after the outbreak of war a number of announcements were made for anyone who had a few hours to spare in the evenings to volunteer for duty as Air Raid Wardens, part-time firemen, fire-watchers and the LDV. These letters LDV stood for Local Defence Volunteers.

To join you went along to your local police station where your name and address were taken and you were told that they would be in touch. As I rode a motorcycle I was put down as a messenger. In due course my first spell of duty was to take my motorcycle and report to someone at a spot on a moorland road at 12 p.m. on the following Saturday.

The location of this meeting place had to be found, but when I did find it and got there it was occupied by two gentlemen. We stayed there until 5.30 a.m. and I understood that these two men were keeping a lookout for parachutists and if they saw anyone I was to walk down to my motorcycle on the roadside and ride off to a local works and phone the Police. I don't remember much being done, but everyone was relieved that no enemy was seen, and so my job as a messenger wasn't needed. We were never called upon to repeat that duty.

There was no uniform at this time, but we wore an armband with the letters LDV printed on which fastened round the arm with two press-studs. We were in a country area and as a number of farmers or their sons joined the LDV it gave us quite a bit of fire power as they brought along their shotguns and, as they all claimed to be able to bring down a running rabbit easily, an enemy soldier seemed like no problem.

Someone seemed to be in charge by this time and meetings were arranged in a local mill yard in the evenings where we did drill and a little keep fit training. Unfortunately this had the effect of reducing our fire power considerably because farmers' sons were not built for knees bend/arms stretched tactics and they weren't much taken up with the idea.

Arthur Fairhurst
BURY, LANCASHIRE

Yes, I certainly remember the Home Guard. We joined on a Sunday morning and I said I was 16 years old and signed up there and then. We were given an armband with LDV on it standing for Local Defence Volunteers or, as we were popularly known, 'Look, Duck and Vanish'. The other comment that we usually got was that 'He who fights and runs away lives to fight another day'. Not on British soil, perhaps, but certainly in other areas of war.

Local farmers and landowners were 'made up' to officers. They were already the 'bosses' of some of the platoon, and of course it was their land and buildings we used to practise our warlike training on. So they had to be in charge.

Approached one 'Captain Mainwaring' type. I came to attention and saluted but my pal Dick just leant on his gun.

'Do you know who I am?' said the captain.

'No. And I don't know as I want,' growled Dick.

End of conversation. It was Dick's land we were on that Sunday morning.

Reginald Underwood
IPSWICH, SUFFOLK

I was in the Local Defence Volunteers in 1940. I was 18 and waiting to go in the army and so decided with my elder brother, who was unfit for the military, to join the LDV.

Near Wellingborough is Sywell Aerodrome, and on the road leading to it we had to patrol both at dusk and dawn and check all vehicles.

One morning I remember we were on the dawn patrol

and we had drawn our rifles and the five rounds of ammunition we were given, together with our arm-bands, the night before. Early in the morning and before light we cycled to the aerodrome which was about three miles away and took up our positions.

I remember a little later on we saw the lights of an approaching car and looking for our torch to wave it up and down we realised then that we had forgotten it. Not to be beat my brother had an idea.

'Take your cycle into the middle of the road, and shine your red rear light at him,' he said.

That was easier said than done. The rear light worked from a dynamo that worked off the rear wheel, so there he was in the middle of the road with his rifle, and me with the back wheel held up in the air and turning the pedals like mad to get a light going to signal the driver. I am pleased to say he stopped.

But I often smile to myself when I think of that scene on a cold winter's morning in 1940. What would have happened if the car decided not to stop.

Or even worse what if it had been THE ENEMY...

Ron Patrick
WELLINGBOROUGH, NORTHAMPTONSHIRE

I was 18 when the war broke out and as a machine tool designer I was in a reserved occupation. Therefore when Anthony Eden called for volunteers for the Local Defence Volunteer force, LDV as it was called before it became the Home Guard, I joined the local town company.

I lived in Oldbury, which is situated between West Bromwich and Dudley. I was the seventh person to join there. You had to report to the Police Station.

The first few months was plain drilling in the police yard. The people who had First War experience or army experience were obviously the ones who became the NCOs.

We had no arms that would work, long Lee-Enfields that were missing vital parts, or short Lee-Enfields that had been sleeved down to .22" bore. These worked but we had no ammunition to use. The old sweats were all for digging trenches in all the open spaces where paratroops could possibly land or where defences could be set up against the invading forces. It didn't make sense to us younger ones when you thought what the Germans had done to the French defences and we had only broken 'non-working' weapons. So a lot of arguments went on in the early days as to the best method of defence. In our young opinion it was to have running battles if possible with mobile forces, but the older generation was so ingrained with trench warfare that they would not accept that concept.

It was not until the LDV became the Home Guard and was mobilised on a Regular Army basis with Regular full-time officers and NCOs that things became more organised.

Eric Gregory
TAMWORTH, STAFFORDSHIRE

I was eight years old when war was declared and I can still remember as if it were yesterday my mother, tears streaming down her face, clutching me to her saying, 'Don't let them take you.'

However, my father who was an ex-First World War veteran joined the LDV which soon became called 'The Look, Duck and Vanish' Brigade. He didn't mind that and he also trained with a brush handle like a good soldier.

Clifford B. Fawcett
NELSON, LANCASHIRE

I n the early days of the war there was a group of men called 'Local Defence Volunteers' (LDVs). I remember my dad coming home in a light brown cotton denim battle-dress suit. It nearly drowned him. He looked more like an escaped convict than a soldier.

On the left arm there was an armband with LDV in big letters. Dad said it stood for 'Look – Duck – and Vanish'. There was little or no equipment, and I remember they used to do their rifle drill with brush handles.

Mrs Rennison (centre) with her parents and baby sister

This was obviously very thirsty work, because it was always followed by a spell at the local pub, which was longer than the actual rifle drill.

Also they used to dig trenches every Sunday morning, which was even more of a thirsty job because that needed all afternoon in the local pub.

Later on they became the Home Guard, and did in fact become quite a smart Home Front defence.

Dad always said that if Hitler had come early in the war we would certainly have won because all his troops would have laughed themselves to death at the sight.

Mrs Mavis Rennison
ROCHDALE, LANCASHIRE

In 1940, after Dunkirk, the risk of enemy landings was felt to be a real possibility. Anyway the idea of a civilian army was very quickly thought out. Retired ex-army officers were contacted to form this force. I lived in a village called Markington, five miles from Ripon in Yorkshire, and worked in a Lime Quarry, and lived in lodgings, for which I paid 30 shillings a week.

Newspapers and radio announced the setting up of what was at that time called the Local Defence Volunteers, and pleaded for men to join it, stating 'your country needs you'. Posters were put up in the village shop and pubs stating that a meeting would be held at 8 p.m. in the 'Yorkshire Hussars' public house. Men in the pubs talked about going along to listen to what was involved by joining. On the night, a chap who was a retired army captain came along and gave a good talk on the urgent need for this force to be formed. At the end of the talk forms were handed out and I think wisely the ex-captain insisted they were filled in at once. You couldn't take them home to fill in later. Anyway 20 chaps signed up at once.

The following Sunday training started. In civvy clothes we paraded in a yard behind the pub, and most important, the pub was set up as our headquarters. We got broom handles to drill with for a short time but in about two months a supply of rather old Lee-Enfield rifles came packed in dirty grease. We all spent our evenings cleaning them.

Bill Hunt was made up to sergeant and I was promoted to corporal. We were then in charge of drilling and guard duties and for manoeuvres done on Sundays when troops from other villages tried to invade us, or we would try to outwit some village and invade them.

I am not sure but I think we got uniforms within six months of joining. Just as well as our clothes were getting worn with creeping through ditches and woods and hedgebacks. Also sleeping out some nights in barns. Don't forget coupons were needed to buy new clothes. New recruits came along and joined when they saw what we did but once in you had difficulty to drop out, as everyone had to do some spare time service, and often the Home Guard, as it now was, was the lesser of two evils.

John H. Scoby
REDCAR, CLEVELAND

I think many people these days think of the Home Guard as a lot of doddering old men. Such was not the case as we had many young men in our lot some of whom were in reserved occupations. Some of the others, like myself, were simply waiting to 'come of age' for the army. Others were just below the physical standards required. At least one of the latter cases that I knew personally was very strong and tough. He later trod the corridors of power and rose to the dizzy height of lance corporal. We did have some who would make a sergeant major's eyes water. One I remember couldn't see the barn never mind hit a barn door. But on the whole we were quite a reasonable force.

Joseph O'Keefe
DUNSTON, GATESHEAD

I was working as a displayman with the City of Cardiff's newly opened CWS emporium, located in the centre of the city. With the evacuation of Dunkirk and the commencement of air activity over South Wales, but very little bombing at this stage of the war, the *South Wales Echo* reported the news that a defence army was to be formed and would be known as the Local Defence Volunteers (LDV).

My pal, Arthur Hockeridge, and myself immediately went down to the famous Cardiff Arms Park, where the first volunteers were to be formed up and organised. Mostly old soldiers from the previous war, but sprinkled with enthusiastic youngsters, there was a melee when potential self-promoted NCOs of the First World War all had a go at drilling us. The whole assembly was chaotic. We had all been issued with khaki armbands with the letters in black (LDV) but it was obvious that the numbers on parade were too much for organisation so we were split up into smaller units. In our case the CWS formed their own unit, the depot being at the massive wholesale building also in the centre of the town.

A couple of shop managers promoted themselves as officers, although lacking any military experience, and some under managers became NCOs. Slowly issues of uniform became available but distinguishable in that the belts and gaiters were leather and we wore the LDV armband and were slowly issued with Remington rifles and 15" bayonets.

Drilling was a disaster and was held on the top of the CWS flat roof. None of the officers or NCOs knew the first thing about drill and so a Regular NCO from the Welsh Regiment was allocated to us. He put us through our drill, saluting, marching, turning, halting, presenting arms, sloping arms, but nothing with which to combat paratroopers who at that time were imminent. We didn't even have ammunition and were left to our own ideas as to what use we would put our bayonets.

At last guard duty was to be performed and this in the very large warehouse of the food part of the CWS complex. This offered us a free meal of bacon and eggs and we were located in the deepest part of the basement. I stood on sentry, *locked* in a food store, in the dark with no means of exit or entry by anyone other than the guard commander. The two hours' guard dragged by leaving me to wonder just what I was meant to do, although I was in the safest area of Britain as far as I was concerned.

Arthur and I were still full of exuberance at being equipped with uniform and rifles. Even if we weren't on

duty, we would don our uniforms and carry our bayonets and then parade through Cardiff, looking for some officer to salute and quickly crossing the road to make sure this involved any officer on that side of the road. Cardiff station was also a good place and the Regular Military Police were obviously nonplussed by such enthusiastic volunteers.

Sundays entailed us marching through town and out to various destinations on the outskirts of Cardiff and in the vicinity of certain public houses, where despite the licensing laws of closure on Sundays, certain older members of the company would manage to obtain a drink from a landlord who thought his pub would thus be stoutly defended if invasion took place.

Bill Hall
SHAFTESBURY, DORSET

On the evening of 14 May 1940 a statement was broadcast that changed the lives and habits of thousands of men in the British Isles. The Secretary of State for War, Anthony Eden, announced that a Home

Defence Force was to be formed and that it would be known as the Local Defence Volunteers, LDV for short, and that this force would be made up of men between the ages of 17–65 and that anyone interested was to report to the local police station.

Within a few hours thousands had offered their services. I was one of those men. At that time I was a 20-year-old farm worker who had registered for military service and was not accepted as I was in a reserved occupation, so I saw this as a chance to do my bit in the defence of my country.

Within 24 hours a meeting had been arranged at the local village hall and a selection committee formed consisting of the local policeman, a retired army captain and a retired sergeant major. I had a fair bit of experience with a sporting gun and also five years' experience of rifle shooting at a nearby rifle club. That seemed to satisfy the selection board and I was duly enrolled.

Within a few days the first parade was called. Everyone was keen to get on with the job, but the majority had no idea at all what would be expected of them. We had no uniforms and no weapons. Some of us had taken our shotguns with us and with these we began to make some progress in our drill.

After a short time our LDV armbands arrived and we really felt we were part of the defence of Britain. As organisation improved both locally and in the county we began to have Regular Army instructions and slowly but surely we began to look like a military unit. After a short time we began to receive our uniforms and then our first rifles. When we were issued with our first uniforms it was wives and sweethearts who came to the rescue. Trousers had to be shortened, overcoats and tunics had to be taken in or let out.

The first rifles we were issued with were Canadian Ross 300. They must have been in store since 1918. Many hours had to be spent with boiling water and cleaning materials before they were clean enough to be taken on parade, but at least we now had rifles and uniforms.

As time went by more weapons and training aids were issued to us. More Regular soldiers were billeted in the area as a result of the evacuation from Dunkirk. We had the benefit of instructors from these units at nearly all our parades and we soon became dab hands at stripping and assembling Tommy Guns and Browning Automatic rifles and it was not long before I was given a couple of stripes and spent a lot of my time going round to other local LDV units giving instructions on various weapons.

At the end of August 1940 the title of Local Defence Volunteers was changed to the Home Guard, on the order of Winston Churchill. New shoulder flashes were issued and the denim uniforms we had originally been issued with were replaced by khaki serge uniforms of the

Regular Army. We were also issued with anti-gas capes, service type gas masks and steel helmets.

Wilfred Hodgson
CONINGSBY, LINCOLN

At first they didn't know what to call our officers so they called them section leaders at first and designated their rank by the use of slim purple bars on the shoulder; one, two or three according to their importance. When we became the Home Guard the bars were removed and they became proper commissioned officers with army shoulder pips.

Our company was stationed in a YMCA building in Kennington Lane. It was purpose built for the task in hand by having dormitories and a large flat roof. During the long summer evenings we were pounded and drilled by our NCOs on that flat roof until we were as smart as any Regular Army unit. The great day arrived when we had our first rifles.

Five American Eddystone rifles in a box smothered in thick grease where I guess they had lain undisturbed since being packed away after the First World War.

We set to cleaning them and it was not long before they arrived in ever increasing numbers until at last we all had one. Some of the rifles were the military version of the Winchester, while some Home Guard units were equipped with Canadian Ross rifles that I reckon dated long before the First World War but they would kill a

34

German paratrooper and that is all that concerned us. Although we were now equipped with guns the ammunition was another matter.

We had been given the role by now of setting an all night guard on the Lambeth and Vauxhall Bridges over the Thames, but as .303 cartridges were in very short supply the two men that were on each bridge had only five cartridges between them. They were sealed up in cellophane and woe betide you if you arrived back at the post with the seal broken and no reason for it. On the centre of each bridge we had a small blockhouse which was equipped with a fixed compass on the parapet so that we could fix a bearing on any bombs or parachute mines we saw landing in the river.

Fred Woolford
ROMFORD, ESSEX

In the beginning, when the Home Guard was voluntary, everyone was keen and accepted the boredom as necessary, as the threat of invasion was very real. Although whether we would have been of any use one can only conjecture, but we were determined and would have had a go to the best of our abilities. When the Home Guard became compulsory and folk who were not in the Forces were drafted in, the atmosphere changed. Guard duty was not readily accepted by all and it made the guard commander's life rather difficult. We were all working men during the day with fire-watching duties during nights we were not on Home Guard duties, so one was permanently tired and could do without too much hassle to get people to do their stint.

Eric Gregory
TAMWORTH, STAFFORDSHIRE

When you write any account of the Local Defence Volunteers (or Home Guard as it later became) you must realise the tremendous spirit and enthusiasm of those early volunteers. We were in fact civilians trying to learn the arts of war, and not much time to do it in. Except for some old timers from World War I, most of us had never handled a rifle before so we were all in the same boat. We were all learners.

As is usually the case this forms a comradeship and a bond between the people concerned, and that was certainly not lacking amongst the men of Dunston Local Defence Volunteers. The day after Sir Anthony Eden asked for volunteers from men aged between 17 and 65, I was around the Police Station signing a form to enlist. Our real concern was parachute troops who had already been used to good effect on the battlefields of Europe.

It was not a new idea, for I can remember people writing to the newspapers asking for civilians to be issued with rifles so that they could help to defend their areas if ever the Germans invaded. The spirit was such that many years later and after the war, one of my old Home Guard sergeants said to me just before he died, 'There will never be the spirit in this country again that we had in those old days of the LDV.'

Joseph O'Keefe
DUNSTON, GATESHEAD

PART II
Becoming Professional

'Any modern viewer of *Dad's Army* would have been surprised, expecting to see a shambles of old men. But what they would have seen was a large body of Home Guards with rifles at the slope in tune with the bands. Our bearing and our smartness brought special applause from the crowds. It even prompted one man to run from the crowd and he shouted to the nearby spectators, "What do you think of 'Old Bill' now then?"'

JOSEPH O'KEEFE, DUNSTON, GATESHEAD

Without any doubt, the finest Home Guard company in England was at Loughborough College, now a university. We were all engineering students, bright, young, finish, well-trained and disciplined by good, ex-Regular Army officers. We paraded every Sunday morning and Thursday evening and we were as keen as mustard. We seriously believed we could have stopped Hitler's crack paratroops and panzers.

Occasionally, 'Intelligence' warned that an invasion was expected, and we would stand-to. One of these scares came just as we were dispersing for the Easter vacation, so our company commander gave us orders to take our gear with us and report to the nearest Home Guard unit.

I joined my parents, who were living in a Norfolk village at that time. The local Home Guard platoon commander was flabbergasted when I looked him up and reported for duty. He said I could join his parade at 1000 hours next Sunday and I duly presented myself, properly dressed, with boots and cap-badge polished, to meet the defenders of the parish.

Honestly, I had never seen or quite imagined such a sight. About 25 men were gathered there, aged from 16 to 66. Most wore battle-dress, some wore great-coats, some wore boots, some had tin hats, some had ammo pouches, a few had the full set of webbing equipment, and a few carried rifles. Most had no sewn titles and flashes on

their sleeves, and hardly any had touched either boot polish or Brasso.

About 20 past ten we were asked to fall in. There was no inspection; the roll was not called. Some arrived even later and just joined the parade without a word.

The lieutenant told us he had planned a lesson in field-craft. We marched – like a flock of sheep – to a bit of rough pasture a half mile away where we stood around, chatting and smoking, while a couple of NCOs demonstrated crawling and the use of cover. Then we shambled back again and dismissed outside one of the village's pubs.

I was disgusted with the whole outfit – the appalling quality of the instruction, the lack of discipline, the absence of effective leadership, the low morale. That pack of yokels couldn't have stood up to a patrol of German Girl Guides. Needless to say I didn't trouble to attend any more of their parades.

John Bevis
ST SAVIOUR, JERSEY

The Home Guard was voluntary until late 1941, when a law was introduced requiring everyone of a particular age to join an approved part-time service. My friend and I thought this was very 'un-British' and we tried to resign. Certainly there was a change in the spirit of the platoon as we considered ourselves rather elitist till then. However, the Home Guard itself was beginning to turn more professional and there were even anti-aircraft guns manned by the Home Guard.

Peter Carter
KNOWLE, BRISTOL

When we were on duty we were paid four shillings and sixpence a night but whether we were on duty or not we went to the post every night as it was our 'home from home' and our club as well. When we came out in the morning most of us cycled straight to work, hung our rifles and bayonets in the workroom or office and put our overalls on over our uniforms. What made us do it? Well, in my case I wanted to protect my mum and sisters (I wasn't too concerned about Dad) and I think it was also the fact that Jerrie thought we were a walkover and we wanted to show him that was not so.

Fred Woolford
ROMFORD, ESSEX

I lived in a small village called Bayston Hill, which was approximately six miles from Shrewsbury. Our company of Home Guard, which was attached to the Fourth Battalion King's Shropshire Light Infantry, consisted of farmers, farmworkers, business people and various other characters.

One of our members was an old colonel named Colonel Gattager. He was about 70 and too old to go into the army but he decided that he would try and do his bit and he came to join our parades.

Two of our sergeants had been in the First World War and they still addressed the old colonel, although he was now only a private, as 'Yes, Colonel' and always called him 'sir'. The old boy always turned up with a cape on and his 12-bore shotgun but after about two years they decided even he was too old to be a member of the Home Guard and reluctantly he had to give it up.

Gerald Cock
STAFFORD, STAFFORDSHIRE

I would like to tell you a wartime memory about the Home Guard or rather the Junior Home Guard. My husband and I were visiting North Wales and during

the day we had been walking in the lanes. As the afternoon drew to a close we knew it was time we made our way home, but suddenly we discovered that we were lost.

We came to a farm-yard where a group of children were playing. Their ages ranged from six to twelve years I should think, and we asked them if they could tell us the way to the bus stop.

They walked away and talked to each other and remember we had been walking all day and so we must have looked very untidy. Also we had a rucksack with our belongings in. Eventually they came back and made a circle around us. A little girl said that if we gave them our identity cards they would tell us.

So we handed over our identity cards and they took them and walked away. They all looked at them very carefully. They must have decided we were not the enemy so they returned them to us. They told us the bus stop was just down the lane and around the corner.

If we had just walked a short distance we would have found it ourselves in any case. I am so pleased we didn't. I have never forgotten that experience and I think they were wonderful. They were well and truly our 'Junior Home Guard'.

Mrs Eveline Cole
GREAT CLACTON, ESSEX

My memories of the Home Guard are as a member of the Army Cadet Force. Prior to leaving school when I was 14 years old we went on a week's camp exercise to Arley Close at Bewdley. On the first Saturday night together with a chap named Steve Robinson we were on guard patrol doing the 12 midnight to 2 a.m. stint. It was teeming with rain and after an hour we were soaked through.

Steve said he had had enough and was going home. I decided to go with him and we put our '202' rifles in a tent and started walking. It took us about six hours to reach Colley Gate where we lived, but no one was awake at my home so I had to knock them up.

Mum and Dad were very surprised to see me back so early and in such a state, and Dad soon had the boiler lit for hot water and then put me in the tin bath for a good soak.

All was well at that time,

but about three weeks later a buff envelope came marked 'OHMS' the contents of which was a summons for my father and I to attend a 'Court of Enquiry' at Halesowen Grammar School. It meant Dad losing a day's pay and he wasn't too pleased about that. The outcome of the enquiry was a fine of 7/6d and discharge from the Cadet Force.

I felt the lash of Dad's belt for the 7/6d fine. Steve had the same punishment.

Four years later I was called up for the Regular Army and on the first day at Norton Barracks I met my old cadet sergeant who was now an army sergeant. He remembered me but that's another story and perhaps I'd better not tell it here.

Lawson Howard Attwood
CRADLEY HEATH, WEST MIDLANDS

I was 16 years old when I arrived home in khaki battle-dress and a .300 Canadian World War I rifle. I had joined the Home Guard and I had an armband to prove it.

My mother was shocked to see the war brought home and I immediately got into trouble. Fortunately the Germans never invaded although we spent many cold nights patrolling our village along the railway line and sleeping our four hours off duty in the weight-man's cabin.

Next day would be work as usual then drill at night in the local school. Later I joined the newly formed Air

Training Corps as well, and also became church organist and choirmaster, so it was a rest to join the RAF later on in the war and only have one job to do.

Our biggest exercise in the Home Guard was to capture the railway bridge taking the LNER traffic across the River Tyne from Newcastle to Carlisle one Sunday morning. When we arrived at Blaydon in a lorry we were told by the adjudicator that we had all been shot by the local platoon hiding around a corner and had to go into a prisoners' compound. It seemed such a waste of time, so my friend and I decided to escape and try to reach the railway bridge.

Peter Carter is standing on the extreme right

We reached the lines and tried to cut through Fisons Fertiliser factory. However, this turned out to be the defenders' headquarters and an officer was chatting to two of his men about football. We crept quietly in, let out a yell and threw a 'grenade' made of sand in a paper bag. They got the shock of their lives and the officer fell backwards into a pile of white phosphates. At the sight of what we had done we slammed the door and dashed out, reaching the railway bridge without any further challenge. We waited ages at that spot to claim victory, but nobody came. In the end we walked back to brag about our success, but someone said it had all fizzled out an hour ago and everybody had adjourned to a pub.

Peter Carter
KNOWLE, BRISTOL

I joined the Home Guard at the age of 14 years and 8 months. To join I actually told them that I was 17 and a half years of age, and they believed me. I was in it until it was disbanded in 1944. I was in C Company of the 52nd Battalion of the Essex Regiment.

All my training I did was in civilian clothes. It took about six months or more to get a uniform. I still have a photo of myself going on Sunday morning parade with rifle, gas mask and steel helmet.

Frank Taylor
ROMFORD, ESSEX

We were a well-kitted out company of Home Guard and we had two uniforms. There was a 'best' uniform for parades and a denim uniform for battle exercises and for working on the lorries. The tunics buttoned up to the neck. It was easy to tell a Home Guard from a soldier by his puttees. Our gaiters or puttees were black leather, very stiff and awkward, whereas a regular soldier's puttees were made of webbing. We didn't have to polish our buttons as they were made of Bakelite and not brass which was a blessing.

We were issued with old .303 Lee-Enfield rifles. They were unsafe to fire live ammunition but all right with blanks. We also had bayonets and gas masks, and my Home Guard gas mask was fine to wear, but I couldn't bear to have my civilian gas mask on as I felt it was suffocating me. We had helmets too. All this equipment had to be taken home and cleaned and kept in our rooms. We made a lot of noise with our hobnail boots in the streets and also getting on and off the trams. We didn't wear our uniforms on social occasions. It just wasn't done. I was also at that time on Fire Guard and when the sirens went I was supposed to don my black helmet and armband and go out to watch for incendiary bombs, but at night I couldn't get up. I was always so sleepy.

Francis A. Dancey
OLDHAM, LANCASHIRE

The clothing issued at first consisted of army overalls that you had to wear over your own clothes. Later we had Regular Army khaki uniforms with ox-blood coloured leather belts and gaiters. As they were made by various manufacturers the colours were of many shades and looked revolting. One was not allowed to change the colour – only polish them. Then the powers that be decided that to make us look a bit more presentable, they would change the colour to black. They did not reissue new leatherwork but ordered us to change the colour ourselves. Black stain was not easily come by. One scoured all shops to find some. Some were lucky. Others were not and had to try to get the equipment black by using black boot polish, which did not cover very well so the various shades of black were almost as bad as the ox-blood colour, until a new issue of proper black was made. One perk of being in the Home Guard in our area was that some bus conductors let you ride free of charge, if you were in uniform, so one tended to wear it more than was strictly necessary.

Armbands were used originally with Home Guard on them as there were no shoulder flashes but these were issued later so we dispensed with the armbands, which were a nuisance as they were not tight. They had a nasty habit of slipping down at the wrong moment.

Eric Gregory
TAMWORTH, STAFFORDSHIRE

I was in the Home Guard for 12 months between the ages of 16 and 17 until I joined the Merchant Navy for the next 14 years. When I first joined we were issued with Remington .303 rifles plus bayonets, which we kept at home. We used to attend the barracks just on odd evenings for training plus every Sunday, as we had full-time jobs during the week.

I worked at a dry cleaner's for a while and I think I had the smartest uniform in the battalion until one of the women employees there realised whose uniform was being pressed every week.

I later progressed to a Lewis gun and I remember coming home from work at the local brickyard and my mother said, 'The sergeant has just been round and he has left something for you on the settee.' It was a brand-new Sten gun. As soon as I had my tea I went round to my pal's house a few doors away to tell him and got another surprise. He was in possession of a Lewis gun. He had been told to learn to strip it and reassemble it blindfolded.

Looking back now it was a silly thing to do, but when we used to go on the firing range on Sundays for practice I used to manage to get hold of a few extra 9mm rounds for the Sten gun. One evening when my pal's parents were out we were shooting at cans on the wall when one of us hit the cast iron drainpipe and we were lucky we weren't hit with the broken pieces that flew off. I can still remember my mate's dad scratching his head and looking at the two-foot gap in the drainpipe. He never did find out what happened.

John L. Burt
SCARBOROUGH, NORTH YORKSHIRE

Our two sergeants were World War One veterans, so knew all about kitting up, drill, etc., once they had accustomed themselves to the 'three ranks' instead of the old time two then 'form fours'. The other NCOs were raw but promoted because of their keenness, awareness and superior intelligence.

When I joined early in 1941 we had, I think, only four World War One American Browning .300 rifles and a few privately owned guns, e.g. sporting guns and .22 rifles. There was then a perfectly good reason for this – the country was still reeling from Dunkirk, where most of our equipment had either been destroyed or left behind. We gradually received obsolete but perfectly effective weapons

from the USA. There were rifles and machine guns, and by 1943 everyone had a rifle and our company had a Browning machine gun and several sub-machine guns. I noted in my diary of 1942 that we might be issued with bayonets fixed on to barrels of piping and our few rifles withdrawn. Fortunately this never took effect. I do remember that our crowd told their officers they would refuse to march through their own town shouldering these 'pikes' as they would never live down the ridicule.

James Frewin
SHERBORNE, DORSET

Our first real experience with rifles, firing one that is, was on the ranges at Botany Bay, beyond the sewage works. But the real shooting we did was at the Holcombe army range where not only were we taught all the firing positions like standing, kneeling and prone stances, but we were actually fired AT. As we crawled under tapes set about 18 inches above the ground, regular soldiers fired over our heads. I can't recall which general in history it was who said, 'By God, Sir, I don't know what they do to the enemy, but they terrify me,' but I can assure you that in those exercises I certainly shared his sentiments.

John Slawson
HEYWOOD, LANCASHIRE

We have all heard of *Dad's Army* but how many people know that women were recruited

– unofficially? As a young clerk in the Air Ministry from 1939–45 I was in a reserved occupation as were the heads of our departments, mostly men in their forties. These men became the officers and other ranks of the Air Ministry Battalion of the Home Guard. We girls had already volunteered for fire-watching and first-aid duties but were longing for the glamour of a uniform so we asked if we too could join the Home Guard. There was no precedent for this and our request was refused at first. However, we had enlisted the sympathy of the officers and with their approval the Air Ministry Auxiliary Section of the Home Guard was formed to provide a back-up for the men.

The only uniform 'Dad's Daughter's Army' was allowed was a navy blue boiler suit, navy 'fore & aft' cap, service tin hat and respirator. This was not our idea of glamour and we soon tailored the boiler suits to fit better, embroidered armbands with AMAS and were ready to go. But to go where?

We paraded weekly and some were detailed to be cooks, some to be signallers. I was one of the latter, to be taught Morse code (or rather to revise it as I had been a Girl Guide) by a redoubtable Sergeant Wright, a Great War veteran. I don't think my di-di-di-da-dits broke any records. My CO both in and out of the office was Captain Arthur Beckess.

The highlight of one summer was a day out with the men on manoeuvres at Hatfield airfield bumping there in an army truck. We were given instruction and allowed to fire service rifles – vicious beasts with a tremendous

Mrs Baker (left) with Janie Imrie from Scotland, 1940

kick; in fact at the first attempt I thought I might have died of shock. Looking back after all these years we were just as funny as the BBC's *Dad's Army*. What a 'job lot' we were. I wonder how much support we could have given in an emergency, a real one. Fortunately this was never put to the test but for us it was a wonderful morale booster and I still have the photographs to prove it really happened.

What I do remember is one night having worked late I had been met at the station by my parents to walk home with me in the blackout. As we walked up a very quiet semi-country road in Epsom, two men leapt out of the bushes and demanded to know 'Friend or Foe'. My mother nearly had a seizure on the spot. My father, an old soldier of the Great War, took it all in his stride but had to admit we did not know the password. We must have looked harmless because we were allowed to pass and go on our way.

Mrs Lois V. Baker
CROYDON, SURREY

I left school at the age of 14. School and home was in the village of Ibstock in Leicestershire and when I left school I went to work at the local Ibstock Brick and Tile Works. The works had a unit of Home Guard of about platoon strength. Some of my workmates, who were a few years older than I, were members, and I used to tag along at parades and weapon training until one day I was asked by the officer in charge if I would like to join the unit.

Can you imagine the excitement of a 14-year-old boy? I'd been issued a uniform and equipment. I was given a sub-machine Sten gun as the rifles issued to the Home Guard were as tall as I was at that time.

So I began training for real with the rest of the platoon and with the various weapons, rifles, machine guns and grenades. To someone of my age it was one long adventure, even on the day we were live grenade throwing. The usual practice was for one man to be put in the pit with the instructor, and throw the live grenade. We would count to four, then duck down in the pit. Then we would return to our positions about 30 yards behind the throwing pit, and wait with the other members of the squad while another man had his turn at throwing the grenade.

One day I was waiting at this position and a grenade had just been thrown and exploded, when by some freak the base cap of the grenade came flying back and actually cut through the shoulder strap of my uniform. Then it buried itself in the ground. The gods certainly smiled on me that day.

Albert Squires
BLACKPOOL, LANCASHIRE

The white cliffs of Dover must have witnessed many strange spectacles, but surely none more strange than that experienced by a Home Guard Coast Artillery team.

At the time I was a Warrant Officer Gunnery Instructor at South Eastern Command headquarters and I found myself roaming the coast from Ramsgate to Dover, Folkestone, Dungeness and beyond, drawing maps and charts, setting up guns, supervising the training of gun teams, organising practice shoots and taking part in the active role of the heavy artillery, commonly referred to as the 'cross channel guns'.

It had been decreed that the Home Guard, a formidable body of men, would assist the Royal Artillery to defend the coast by manning the six-foot naval guns which were to be seen on the promenades of the coastal towns. This would allow the army gunners to take on a more active role in the field.

Some of the Home Guard gunners had served in the forces during the First World War and one of them proudly displayed to anyone who doubted his efficiency a certificate to the effect that he was a qualified gun-layer in 1904. In 1914 the same man had manned the large guns commanding the heights above Dover and had no doubt seen the Fort Record Book, which held the important items affecting the Battery. It had an item in 1914: 'Fence and gate to landward side repaired', followed by the laconic entry 'Hostilities commenced'. News must have been rather sparse for the next entry was in 1918 'Hostilities ceased' followed by 'Repainted fence and gate'.

Training of the Home Guard duly began and the batteries echoed with the sounds of 'Take post', 'Detachment rear' and now and then 'Oh dear me' when a 100-pound shell accidentally dropped on an innocent toe. Finally, at long last we realised that they were good. Really good. They required only the final accolade: a live shoot.

Coast artillery rarely fired in anger, the Malta six pounders and the heavy Dover guns providing the rare opportunities. So to test the efficiency of the gun teams we would take floating targets into the Channel and practise firing shells at them as they were towed at speed past the battery. The noise was incredibly loud and we

had many complaints from irate local residents, particularly as the most popular time for firing was on Sunday mornings.

It was on such a Sunday morning that, acting as gun critic on number one gun in a Ramsgate Battery, I welcomed the Home Guard on to the platform and they proceeded to ensure that everything was prepared for action. The rammer was fitted with a circular brush and sponge on the end and during action was dipped into a large round bucket of water after the two men had rammed home the shell. It remained in the bucket until the gun had fired and the breech was opened, when it would be taken out and, as the next shell was rammed home, the water on the brush and sponge would douse any smouldering remnants before the next charge of cordite was inserted.

On this occasion we began firing. 'Ready', 'On', 'Set'; the commands came quickly and the gun was fired, then repeated over and over again. But when the fourth shell winged its way towards the target, in addition an object hurtled through the air to descend in the sea just below low water mark. We were puzzled.

My first thought was that it must have been the metal driving band on the shell that had been stripped off. As I pondered on this I saw the chief man on the rammer lift it out of the bucket and look with disbelief at the tip. There was no sponge or brush and, in fact, the top portion of the rammer had completely vanished.

The gunner looked at the rammer. Then he looked at me. He looked into the water bucket, hoping to discover something in the murky depths, and finally he looked up the bore of the gun in the hope that somehow it would still be there. A forlorn hope indeed. It was then that he looked at me again. A look of despair as he realised the enormity of what he, and the gun team, had done. They had *fired the rammer.*

I do not remember the subsequent events very clearly. By the time we had obtained a spare rammer the shoot was finished and soon I was sitting by the side of my driver being conveyed with all speed from the scene. But for some time afterwards I would see, in idle moments, the look of utter bafflement on the gunner's face when he first realised that his rammer had been spirited away by some unknown but malevolent force.

Wilfred Ellis
STEETON, WEST YORKSHIRE

Conditions in the Isle of Man were different from those in England. Not only did we have Army, Navy and Air Force units here but also tens of thousands of enemy civilian internees, both male and female. We also had prisoners of war, and Moseley's British Fascists interned here. Whenever someone escaped, the Home Guard had to double the guard for places that were at risk of sabotage and also the harbours. This, as our numbers diminished, proved to be a great burden to us.

On the other hand, the Manx Home Guard had the advantage of being trained by some of the best Instructors in the three Services. How many Home Guards there were in the Isle of Man I cannot remember. However, there were four active Companies together with head-quarters and Signals. It must also be remembered that most Home Guard experiences consisted of five years of boring guard duty and, tired from lack of sleep, having to go to work the next morning.

The only breaks were the exercises with the Regulars. We also enjoyed the visits to the Ranges for weapon training. Most of the Home Guard will have now fallen on the Great Parade Ground in the sky. However, it will give me great pleasure to write to you my experiences of those years.

The first is a long kept secret. We had a Regular Officer Cadet Training unit on the island. The Home Guard officers, one of which I had now become, were invited to witness the cadets taking part in a night-time river crossing. The widest river on the island being only about 25 feet wide, the O.C.T.U. decided to cross one of our reservoirs.

To make it realistic they set up machine guns to fire tracer bullets from the upstream end of the reservoir into the wall of the dam at the other end. The machine guns were fixed so that the stream of bullets would be well clear of those attempting to cross over. To add to the reality, a rowing boat manned by several sergeants of the training school was to circle the reservoir to throw over the stern small explosive charges. These were to make a bang and flash and throw up a column of water to simulate enemy mortar fire.

The Home Guard officers took up position on the bank. In the darkness we heard the cadets inflate their rubber boat and set off across the dam. They were then supposed to be 'discovered' by the enemy. These fired off parachute flares which turned night into day.

All hell broke loose. The machine guns opened up, tracer bullets crossed the length of the reservoir, and smashed into the wall of the dam at the other end. Explosions and columns of water appeared well to the stern of the rowing boat.

Then just as one of the flares went out there was a terrific explosion. All was dark for a few moments when another flare went up and we saw to our horror that where the rowing boat had been there was now only a circle of foam on the water.

We subsequently learned that the previous flare on its parachute had accidentally landed in the boat and detonated all the explosives that had been on board. When we of the Home Guard reached our headquarters we had to await the arrival of an O.C.T.U. officer who swore us all to secrecy.

Then there is my story of what I call 'unfair shares'. After Crete had been captured by German paratroops, the RAF were very concerned about the defence of their airfields. When maps were found in Germany after the war, the Isle of Man was shown to be seriously considered by the enemy as an ideal base from which to attack the west coast of England, if only as a diversion. It also had the advantage of containing many prisoners of war who could be released and armed.

The RAF airfield at Jurby was, after the experience of Crete, thought to be very vulnerable to airborne attack. The Home Guard were probably considered to be of small use to defend it but a most useful body to take on the role of German paratroops. We could attack it and so provide a useful way of testing the defences.

The required number set off from Douglas on a Victorian steam railway. This was probably to save petrol which was in short supply. As the driver of the engine was a Home Guard himself he was determined to show what he could do. We must have reached at least 40 miles an hour going downhill.

We had a most interesting if exhausting afternoon,

putting in several previously arranged attacks. We were never told what the umpire had to say about us. When we had finished we were afforded RAF hospitality. I had just reached the exalted rank of sergeant. My friend Jim, however, had become an officer. So the officers were invited to the Officers' Mess. The sergeants were invited to the Sergeants' Mess, and all the ranks to the appropriate airfield mess. I had the most wonderful meal that I had had since the rationing began.

'Have another plateful of ham and eggs, sergeant.'

'What about another piece of apple pie or cake?'

When we got back to our train I said to Jim, 'What a marvellous meal.'

'What meal?' he said.

'All the ham and eggs and cake,' I replied.

'Well, all we had in the Officers' Mess was afternoon tea,' he said.

My reply was simple, 'Well, you would become an officer.'

W. Lockington Marshall
BALDRINE, ISLE OF MAN

I suffered a setback in health and after some months in 'military' hospitals I was discharged on medical grounds. Notwithstanding this I volunteered to join the Home Guard, ostensibly in a platoon to guard the newly built and operational Power Station at Little Barford, St Neots, Huntingdonshire.

But my work fellows there and I soon found ourselves chasing around the St Neots area with the rest of the local unit. Then a few months later I returned to live and work in London and quite literally talked ('conned') my way into a transfer into a 'being formed' unit of Home Guard to man the AA [Anti-Aircraft] sites in and around London. I felt happier and involved again.

Within a few weeks of being classified as operational I had two stripes on my arm and in even less time I exchanged them for white tapes and my shoulder straps – Officer Cadet. After several weeks of tough time-absorbing duties (I had a responsible daytime job in the City and lived many miles away with a difficult journey route to and from the gun site to my home), I often 'clocked' more duty hours in those periods of the service in less than a month than we did in our pre-war year in the Territorial Army.

To continue: after much training from army personnel I was commissioned as a Second Lieutenant but I did not follow others 'outside' on to the gun site but was one of six (eight was the site target and requirement) for further intensive training as Plotting officers. As such we saw a fair amount of action against German raiders in the air and received some on site from them. Later I became one of only a dozen or so throughout the UK who became Tactical Control officers. We were classified 'operational' and able to take charge of the total function of the site, including RA [Royal Artillery] and ATS [Auxiliary Territorial Service] Officers and ranks, as well as some 150 or more Home Guard on duty each night, with a potential salvo of 120 AA shells.

Home Guards were on all-night duty, one in eight. Most of ours were dockers as 'coincidentally' our site was by the then extensive Thameside Docks in and around the West Ham area. We plotting officers did one night in six.

Len Barton
WINGHAM, KENT

One cold winter's day we embarked on a journey to a range in Northumberland. The ground was laced with patches of thin snow, and it was very cold. We had been told we were going to be dive-bombed. This was supposed to learn us not to be frightened by the noise. We were supposed to stand up to it all and fire back. I made a mental note that if it came to the real thing I would be the first in the nearest slit trench.

As it happened, by the time our bus got us there it was all over. But we did see a demonstration of an anti-aircraft device. This was a rocket with a huge coil of cable wire attached. When the rocket was fired in the path of enemy bombers it roared into the sky trailing the whipping, lashing cable behind it. I tell you I didn't fancy getting my bootlaces caught in that monster.

Joseph O'Keefe
DUNSTON, GATESHEAD

We did quite a few night schemes designed to help our RAF bomber crews. The general idea was for the air crews to be taken by night in blacked-out lorries miles away from their bomber stations and then dropped in the countryside and left to find their way back by means of compass and without being captured. We, the Home Guard, were spread out across country to prevent this and to capture them. I suppose the thought behind this was to give them some practice if they were actually shot down on a raid.

I remember that the area of one such scheme was near the A446 between Ibstock and Hinckley, close to Osbaston Hall, now the Guinness family residence. I don't remember capturing any airmen, but I do remember being very tired at work next day as we were still required to work normal shifts after these night operations.

Albert Squires
BLACKPOOL, LANCASHIRE

Every Sunday morning we were required to attend parade and after a session of drilling on the parade ground, plus inspection by the commanding officer, we usually went to the nearby countryside for field exercises.

Here mock battles were staged usually in wooded country and as I was familiar with radios I carried a walkie-talkie radio to keep in communication with squads that were 'on our side'. One Sunday we were taken by coach to Bisley Rifle Ranges in Surrey, a nice change from the normal parade. Here, in groups of six at a time, we had to lay full length on the ground and fire five shots at the targets. I had never fired a gun before but with the good eyesight that I had at that time I managed to score three bulls and two inners, much to the surprise of the sergeant in charge.

I well remember that for the rest of that day I found it difficult to hear. Those First World War rifles that we were using, apart from having a kick like a mule, gave a very loud explosion with each shot. At least I had the satisfaction of knowing that I could shoot straight.

Cyril Bird
FRIMLEY, SURREY

The American guns were a .300 calibre as opposed to our .303 but were longer and had more power so they gave a bigger kickback when fired. It was important to get the bolt right down and locked before firing otherwise it had a nasty habit of kicking back. One man was left-eyed and could not fire the rifle in the normal way. He had to put his left eye at the sights, which brought his right cheek over the bolt. Once he did not lock the bolt and the kickback pushed the bolt through his right cheek.

Eric Gregory
TAMWORTH, STAFFORDSHIRE

An example of the hidden dangers in the Home Guard can be given by an experience of mine while on the rifle range. We had been taken there for training, and when it came my turn to fire I laid down with the others and the order came to commence firing. I aimed at six o'clock on the bull's eye, and I took the first pressure on the trigger and was just going to fire when the figure of an old civilian rose from the target pit and covering the bull's eye proceeded to adjust my target. I was aimed right in the centre of his back and ready to fire when just as quickly he sank back under cover. He had been a split second from death. All soldiers know that once the order to fire is given you do not put your head above the trench to adjust a target. It can be decidedly dangerous for your health.

Joseph O'Keefe
DUNSTON, GATESHEAD

I t is easy to forget the underlying seriousness of the Home Guard's activities as we laugh now at the antics of *Dad's Army* on television. Indeed the programme's title has become almost a derisive cliché in our modern language, however kindly it is meant.

It is not hard to understand how this has come about for there can be few Home Guard platoons that did not have a section that almost exactly mirrors the characters featured prominently in the Warmington-on-Sea outfit. Mine certainly did. We had a Pike, a Godfrey and a Mainwaring and several others who could double for the remainder of the TV leads, with just a little imagination.

But as I have implied at the start, it was not all that funny a business at the time. Today I almost marvel to think that most of us at that time were prepared to sell our lives dearly in the defence of our country had the threatened invasion come. It was a time of strange juxtapositions, deadly earnestness combined with lots of unconscious humour, only realised in retrospect very often.

My own experiences took place before I was old enough to go into the army proper. Apart from the occasional exercise or scheme, which for us were usually boring hanging-about affairs on a Sunday, our time was mainly taken up with foot drill, arms drill and weapon training, with periodic all night guard-cum-fire-watching stint at our school building headquarters. Occasionally we would have a large Battalion Parade to attend where we could show off our drill and marching skills.

Tom Plumley (second from right) with rope and dagger.
He says he wasn't standing on the kerb like the others!

It was not long before five of us younger ones obtained permission to form a Commando Section. Released from the more orthodox duties we practised creeping up and attacking from behind, scaling walls, disarming sentries, and all kinds of unarmed combat. We attended a Regular Army unit stationed nearby where the Instructor was one Archie MacCauley, a professional footballer, who later went on to captain Arsenal and Scotland. Invited to attack him, he quickly threw me to the ground and put an armlock on me. I was surprised at how easy I could do the same to him once I knew how. We discovered all sorts of ways to maim, or even kill, with such simple items as a knife, a piece of wire, or the rim of a tin hat.

At our next big exercise, involving all the local Home Guard units and some Regular Army troops, we resolved to put some of our hard-won skills into practice and justify our existence as an independent section. Put briefly, the plan was to surreptitiously board an early morning goods train that would carry us right into the centre of the town, which was being held by the 'enemy'. From observations made over quite a period, we knew a point on the line where this particular train always slowed to a little more than walking pace, and on the great day we were there, ready and waiting.

Excitement rose as, with ear pressed to rail, we could detect the train's approach. Suddenly it appeared and just as suddenly it had gone, disappearing at a high rate of knots into the early morning mist. Either our 'intelligence' was wrong or the driver, for reasons we never knew, had chosen this particular day to go at a speed that ruled out any attempt to board it illegally. The train was the key to our plot. Without it we were sunk.

In glum dismay we had to abandon our daring plans for infiltration, at least for this time, but I am sure that but for that fifth columnist train driver…

I have enclosed a photograph of our five-man Commando Section, and very menacing I think we look. I now clean fish with the wicked-looking knife I am wearing.

Tom Plumley
KINGSTHORPE, NORTHAMPTON

In July [1940] our name was changed to the grand title of Home Guard and gradually we were issued with denim suits, which were the overalls of the army. Few of these suits fitted and we must have looked a motley crowd. However, when we started to get the real serge battle dress, we began to take on the image of a real force.

We had a few rifles in the early days and as one patrol returned, they were handed over to the next pair on duty, and so on, together with five rounds of ammunition. Looking back it seems rather amazing that 17-year-olds were walking around armed, and yet I cannot recall any accidents or misuse of our powers. One wonders if youth would be so responsible today? The first time we went to the Bisley firing ranges I, like many others, felt nervous. We had been warned of the 'kick' of the rifle but in the event I had the top score of eight bulls and two inners at 200 yards, and repeated the feat a few days later on a miniature range. Yet I never became an outstanding shot in my regiment.

Roy Elmer
WINDSOR, BERKSHIRE

When I was a member of the Home Guard it was in Northern Ireland. We were a transport company, the only one I believe in Northern Ireland. We transported other companies around the six counties and we had Thornycroft lorries. They were old, hard to maintain and even harder to drive.

Some of us, including me, couldn't drive, so we were taken out on the country roads for driving lessons. I can particularly remember we had great difficulty in double 'de-clutching' to change gear. One day when I was having a lesson an American convoy of trucks headed by a vehicle with a flag came flying round the bend of a country road completely on the wrong side. I panicked. Fortunately my instructor grabbed the wheel and avoided the leading vehicle but it put me off driving and afterwards I just cleaned and helped to maintain the lorries. We were based in the grounds of a big estate outside Belfast. The lorries were parked under the trees, and we had the use of the various buildings for stores and a workshop. Our .22 rifle range was also there. We did our training at this camp at weekends.

On Wednesday nights we paraded on the top floor of a large warehouse near the docks and drilled there. Our drill sergeant was a First World War drill instructor and he drilled us in ranks of four instead of three, and some of the rifle drill was different, as we found out later when some of us joined the Regular Forces.

We were a very young company, mostly in our teens and early twenties. I was 19. Our platoon sergeant was 24 and looked like Richard Todd. We had a lance corporal who was only 17 and a half. He got his stripe because he was halfway through his motor mechanics apprenticeship.

Northern Ireland didn't have conscription during the war because of the difficulties with the border and the neutral Free State. So all who joined the forces were volunteers, from the south of the border as well as the north. Each Wednesday night was recruiting

night for the Home Guard. Also a list of names was read out of those who had joined the forces. Names of those ex-Home Guard members who were reported missing or presumed dead were also read out which really shook me.

Francis A. Dancey
OLDHAM, LANCASHIRE

Night exercises in local fields, being trained to crawl on your stomach as you approached a farmhouse, were fraught with danger from large thistles and cowpats, not to mention bulls and farm dogs, some of which did not take kindly to being disturbed at night and would have a go at you, sometimes very painfully. Plus an irate farmer coming out and getting at you for disturbing cattle and his sheep, playing 'silly buggers' as he called it. Some farmers, in fact, carried shotguns, fearing that poachers were after their cattle, and would let fly with it before finding out what was going on, so one had to be quick and identify oneself before he could do so; some near squeaks were had.

Eric Gregory
TAMWORTH, STAFFORDSHIRE

During the dark nights we would have lectures or training in the lecture hall. The heavy machine gun sections would be set up in one corner, sometimes practising with their eyes blindfolded. One exercise was guessing ranges of certain objects, and for this we were given a wide panoramic vision of a country scene. From this you had to guess the range of certain places, for instance 200 yards to the small tree in the field, 400 yards to the stream, 600 yards to the farmhouse and so on.

One night we were being taught how to disarm the enemy of his rifle and bayonet if he lunged at you. With your left hand you deflected the bayonet one side, brought your right foot forward and grasping his rifle at the top and bottom you were then supposed to wrench it from his grip. The idea was that you then introduced yourself to him with a blow to his jaw with the butt of his rifle. Of course whether the German agreed with this plan was a different matter.

One night the sergeant major was putting us through this drill and making a good job of it. Gaining confidence he encouraged us to be more realistic, and put more life into it, but his martial spirit dimmed when one young warrior came at him like an express train and nearly pinned him to the wall. And thus endeth this lesson.

Joseph O'Keefe
DUNSTON, GATESHEAD

Two aircraft collided over our village, and I actually saw it happen. Both of the men were saved, and one of the planes crashed near to our village.

I remember we had a man in the village called Ellit Doughty who lived almost straight opposite our house, and he was also at his gate when the planes collided. He dashed into his house, grabbed his rifle and fixed his bayonet. He had no ammunition, but in his short sleeves with no coat on he ran straight down the path, rifle and bayonet pointed straight forward. Straight down a jitty he went, across the fields and apparently ran about half of a mile to the plane to make himself useful by keeping everyone away until the police and the Air Force people arrived.

The funny part of this episode was not only the laugh in the village at Mr Doughty dashing across the fields like that, it was also the fact that poor Mr Doughty was then ordered to stay and guard the wreckage even after everybody else had gone home to bed.

J. N. Marriott
GRANTHAM, LINCOLNSHIRE

As time went on we were eventually issued with rifles and with uniforms and called upon to attend parades on certain evenings and on Sunday mornings. Posts on the edge of our area were set up as lookout posts and in the reservoir area where the local water works were situated. These posts usually consisted of an old wooden hut which was equipped with two old spring mattresses. Three or four of the unit would arrive at nine o'clock and stay all night until 6 a.m. Sleep, of course, was out of the question despite the spring mattresses because somebody always seemed to be popping in and out all night having a look round.

Several Sundays were spent on the rifle range. In time a number of men were drafted into a headquarters platoon, training with the Regular Army on courses at weekends. Each course extended for 12 weekends. The training was then passed on to each platoon in the company at following weekends and hopefully the information given was taken in.

Arthur Fairhurst
BURY, LANCASHIRE

[Eventually] we got real hand grenades, which were the M36. We had stripped and cleaned and thrown the dummy models for some time, and we knew that the Sunday morning parade that week was going to use live bombs for the first time. It was a wet morning. I was a lance corporal and keen and so it was arranged that I would go forward with the officer and each squaddy in turn would then throw the grenades from one gravel pit into another. These were about 10 yards away and we were in a protected area about six to eight feet high.

So we went through the drill and Ronnie drew out the pin, turned to the parapet and heaved with quite a bit of effort. Of course you try to get live grenades as far away as possible, but his foot slipped in the muddy conditions, and the bomb landed against the far wall instead of going over it. Slowly it then rolled back down the ground towards us and the officer made a bit of a move to pick it up, but sensibly changed his mind.

I shouted 'Down' and so did our Captain Burke, and down we went as flat as possible. As the four-second fuse ended, the bomb went off about two feet above us where it had rolled and lodged. Ron had turned and got bowled over in the process, and he said he thought he had been kicked in the back. But when he got home he had a piece of shrapnel in his back just under the skin, and by his spine. It had gone through his top coat belt, and the rest of his clothes. Truly it was a near disaster. The senior officers were not too pleased either. They had dived into the mud on the command 'Down'.

Reginald Underwood
IPSWICH, SUFFOLK

My brother Stanley and I went to join the 10th County of London Home Guard, which was at

my old Junior School in Grafton Road. We both lied about our ages to get in. I said I was 19, and Stan said he was 18. He was actually 15 at the time. The sergeant who signed us on knew we were under age. It was fairly obvious. However, he let us join telling us we would have to join the Signal Section after we had finished our basic training. After that they gave us a rifle which had the old 18-inch bayonet on it. They towered above us, and everyone in the room burst out laughing. Anyhow we both passed our rifle and foot drill test, and we also went to Bisley Rifle Range and I remember firing 20 shots from our BIG rifles. They were old American World War One type. After that we started our signals training, learning Morse code, phonetic alphabet, telephone and radio procedures, and we passed all of our tests. I was then detailed to A Company, Signal Section. Stan was sent to C Company.

Bear in mind that all this time I was only 16 and Stan was only 15. But we stayed in the Home Guard until I was called up into the army when I was 18 where I was trained as tank crew at Bovington and Barnard Castle. I was then sent to Worthing to join the 3rd County of London Yeomanry, and I landed on the Normandy beaches in 1944 as a tank gunner. But thereby lies another story.

George Evan Scofield
CLACTON ON SEA, ESSEX

I met an old friend of mine quite accidentally in the street one day. He was Ronnie Twizell and I hadn't seen him for ages and naturally we had plenty to chat about. In the past we had been in the habit of popping along to each other's houses, about five or six minutes away, partly to have something of a 'jam session' with our guitars. However, during our conversation I mentioned that I was a part-time Special and that I was somewhat fed up with it. I had him laughing when I described our onerous duties when on the beat and how I was losing too much money playing snooker at the club (the loser paid for the use of the table, 3d I believe). Being a beginner I usually got 'slammed' but I must confess I used to enjoy the game, win or lose.

Anyway Ronnie in return told me that he was serving in the Home Guard and that the amenities were marvellous. They were stationed at Northfield Drill Hall and the hall had a nice big stage complete with piano and why didn't I pack the Specials job in and join his mob and we could entertain the lads at night playing our guitars – maybe form a small band with himself on piano. And there was also a nice canteen.

'But hey,' I interrupted him, 'you surely don't all go on duty to sit around playing or listening to musical instruments?'

'Well no, we go down to the gun park for half an hour or so practice – nothing to it – and the rest of the night is left to ourselves.' Music, play cards, play the only gambling game allowed in the British Army (so we were informed) namely 'housey, housey' (more popularly known as 'Bingo').

Really he made Northfield sound very much like a Butlins holiday camp with a touch of Las Vegas thrown in. He would have made a good salesman would Ron, adept at boosting the amenities whilst shading the anomalies. I discovered later that there were one or two things he had forgotten to mention. Suffice to say that according to Ronnie, life in the AA Battery at Northfield was roses, roses all the way. However, I took his advice and paid a visit to Northfield Drill Hall where in no time at all I joined the AA and was 'kitted out' with a real uniform.

We were also issued with heavy army boots but as a special concession we were allowed to wear our own shoes if we wished. Most of us accepted the heavy boots as they were very useful for work in the shipyards.

The Regular Army sergeant who was in charge of the 'kitting out' parade had a marvellous method (I think) of testing the army issue type of gas mask. A few of us would be lined up in single file, gas masks on, then he

Mrs Jean Davison's father

would walk slowly along the line and as he came level with the 'rookie' he would say a few words to him, receive a mumbled reply and suddenly grab and squeeze the tube leading from the chest to the face mask. My goodness, he could just as well have grabbed you by the throat, which in effect he had done for he had squeezed off your air supply. Not only did he prove the effectiveness of the mask but he had also given each and every one of us a practical example of what it must feel like to choke to death. Mind, it was a very funny sight watching the antics and contortions of the *other* lads when it came to their turn.

Sent in by Mrs Jean S. Davison
SOUTH SHIELDS, TYNE AND WEAR
IT WAS WRITTEN BY HER FATHER WHO DIED IN 1984

Mablethorpe Platoon regarded itself as a cut above the rest, having old soldiers like Lieutenant John Manning (wounded three times in the First World War), Sergeant Jack Horton, who came back with one arm missing and was an expert with a Vickers machine gun, and Captain Straw, who lost a leg. Most of the running around was done by the 16 or 17 year olds like myself until our turn came to join up with the other Regulars.

Sergeant Jack Horton was a true professional who had probably mown down more Germans with his Vickers machine gun in France than the makers of *Dad's Army* had ever seen whilst lazing round the swimming pools of Tenerife. But he was too quiet and unassuming to say so. When he was given command of an important crossroads north of Mablethorpe, Stain Lane, he very soon worked out the fields of fire for his machine gun; co-opted a nearby farmer on to the strength, who was rewarded by finding his spare room knee deep in ammunition boxes. With the rest of the detachment in support armed with Ross rifles, Browning Automatic rifles, Phosphorus bombs, Mills bombs, Blacker Bombards, etc., any lightly armed enemy force would have been in for a nasty surprise.

We went on parade one evening a week and every Sunday morning, the Louth Hotel ballroom being a convenient place for winter evenings spent on lectures, bayonet practice, aircraft recognition, first aid, keep fit, etc. The Home Guard held a dance there in aid of something or other which was very well attended by the Regular Army. The bar did a roaring trade and everything went with a real swing. Unfortunately, when we went to collect our warm, new army overcoats from the cloakroom, quite a few were missing, giving rise to the joke by Lieutenant Manning 'the Home Guard is going to hold another dance to get its coats back'.

After much practice at 'bowling' hand grenades, we were marched up to North End into a breezeblock building for the real thing. The Army Lieutenant Instructor showed us how to clean the storage grease from each Mills bomb and insert a U-shaped detonator with the utmost care. Posting a sentry, with the instruction 'let no one pass you, not even Lord Gort', we climbed the sandhills and one man went forward with the instructor into a small pit overlooking a large sandy hollow.

'Prepare to throw', the pin is pulled out and the right hand, securely holding the bomb and handle together, is swung back. 'Throw', and the bomb goes up into the air, the handle flies off and the seven second fuse starts to burn. 'Watch it smoke' was the next order, as smoke curled up from the cricket ball sized bomb laying there in the sand.

'DOWN' was quickly acted upon and the Instructor prostrated himself upon the thrower before the explosion. We had it dinned into us that anyone dropping a bomb accidentally must throw themselves upon the bomb to save their comrades. This did not go down very well later on when I told my father, because he had other plans for his son and heir.

Albert John Freeman
MABLETHORPE, LINCOLNSHIRE

Sunday morning exercises gave us despatch riders the opportunity to ride around pretty fast as conditions allowed.

In the area were set up along most roads a series of tall burners that were filled with any type of used oil so that when they were lit, provided lots of dense smoke. These were used on moonlit nights to put a smoke screen over the area and blank out targets for the German bombers. The stench was terrible but one put up with it, if it kept the bombs away. One morning I was going too fast for the bends in the road, ran up the gutter and came off the bike. My foot became hooked under the handlebars so as the bike slid down the road it pulled me with it. My shoulders were on the pavement in the line of the smoke screen canisters and knocked quite a few over before I came to rest. Oil was all over the place and me. We had just been issued with Regular Army riding outfits consisting of waterproof breeches, short riding coats and crash helmets. So I christened my crash hat amongst the steel canisters. My backside was on the tarmac of the road and as I slid along it wore a hole in my nice new riding breeches. In fact the hole, about one and a half inches in diameter, went through my breeches, my army trousers, my underpants and I stopped just in time to stop flesh being taken.

Eric Gregory
TAMWORTH, STAFFORDSHIRE

We were attached to a section in the neighbouring town of Uxbridge and we had to cycle over there to attend parades at least twice a week and at weekends. This meant that we had to cycle the three and a half miles in the 'blackout', a somewhat perilous undertaking, as the only light allowed in the front was the light from the lower half of an ordinary cycle lamp. The upper half was blacked out.

On a dark, wet or foggy night (and fog was commonplace then being a low lying district plus universal coal fires), it was very difficult to see pedestrians, who habitually walked in the road as it was easier to use the road than uneven pavement in the dark.

James Frewin
SHERBORNE, DORSET

Field exercises were a great adventure. As I was only 16 years old my task was that of a messenger boy to Lieutenant Holton. I was to take messages through 'enemy lines' to headquarters which to me seemed quite an adventure. Cycle lamp batteries of course were not available, so we had to use carbide lamps. Often when

Harold Guest (back row, second from left)

cycling home from duty at night the light used to blow out, and sure enough the same local constable always seemed to be waiting for me. I always used to give him the same excuse – the lamp had blown out. And he always used to feel it and if it was warm I was okay but if it wasn't I had my name taken.

Harold G. Guest
WELLINGBOROUGH, NORTHAMPTONSHIRE

We were made up of farm workers, quarry men, railwaymen, postmen, munitions workers, etc. We had, at the peak, 28 men. We travelled to the army depot at Ripon for rifle training and range shooting and had the army NCOs train us in machine guns, mortars and hand grenades, going mainly on a Sunday by private hire bus. Petrol was strictly rationed but you did get an allowance for army duties in addition to your normal ration.

We had a post at Hob Hill, a fairly steep grass hill with a stone barn on top. We had to take turns with other villages to man a guard on this hill. Three men and an NCO were on duty each night. I used to be in charge and had to wake up every two hours to make sure the guard was changed and to check the sentry was awake. Our captain and his friends often used to try to sneak up on us but were always stopped and challenged: 'Halt Who Goes There?'

I had one chap, about 45, a farm labourer who, when on guard, would have just as soon fired on them as challenge them. In fact, we expected it to happen some day. This chap also used to set snares when on guard duty and we always took home a rabbit or two each, a welcome to my landlady with meat ration very tight.

John H. Scoby
REDCAR, CLEVELAND

Going back to the danger of hidden training I remember when I threw my first grenade. We had been led down to the firing point and while everyone sat back out of danger the first 'victim' took his place in the firing trench with an NCO. We knew what to do in theory, but we were given a quick run through of the drill for throwing. 'Grenade in right hand, withdraw firing pin with the left hand, lob the grenade over head, like bowling a cricket ball.' It was a method I've never liked.

I think many men have made the same mistake as I did. As my arm came over my head I 'clawed' the bomb down. The NCO roared 'Get down' as he dragged me to the bottom of the trench and the bomb exploded a few feet in front of the weapons pit. 'Are you trying to kill me, lad?' said the NCO as I slunk back red-faced to join my fellow warriors. It wasn't a very heartening encouragement for the next man to throw.

Another event I remember is when we had a full day's training programme in Gibside Estate. We arrived there by bus and were casually disembarking in a country lane near the entrance to Gibside when our little world was shattered as giant thunder flashes burst amongst us. Apparently we had been ambushed. Orders were shouted and soon we were taking action against our 'invaders'. This was to let us see we were here to learn, and not for the pleasant day outing we had expected.

This was the day we had our first casualty. It was a minor wound inflicted on the fair brow of 'Tucker'

Johnson. We had gathered around a deep hole in the ground and our explosives expert on the job was Mr Iredale, who was a local chemist. In his hand he held a 'blast' bomb. 'This is a blast bomb,' he said, 'and when I throw it you will see a tape unravel itself. When you see that happening that's when you duck behind the parapet and fast.'

We were all jammed shoulder to shoulder peering into the pit. Tucker's face was looking right over my shoulder when the bomb was thrown. The tape started to unravel, and having a fine sense of preservation as regards my skin, I hit the deck. When we got to our feet Tucker had a trickle of blood from his forehead. Curiosity had got the better of him and he had 'wanted to see what happened'. I don't think it bothered him much. He was built like a tank and you would have had to hit him with the bomb to have got him down.

I think it was on this course at Gibside that I saw a very impressive display of camouflage. We were taken to some fields and asked if we could see anything unusual. We stood looking for a while and couldn't see anything out of the ordinary. Just grass and shrubs. Then an officer blew a whistle and a group of men stood up right in front of our eyes. They must have been members of some of the other local Home Guard units.

Joseph O'Keefe
DUNSTON, GATESHEAD

One day a strange piece of equipment arrived, a piece of piping about six feet and a tripod of tubing on which the piping was placed, swivelled and had a rubber bicycle handlebar grip at the end of the control for aiming. We also had a case of bottles, which we were told were Molotov Cocktails. When placed in the breech, we added a small cardboard canister, closed the breech and placed a small cartridge on the outside of the breech, which now made it a tank killer with a range of about a hundred feet. We were never allowed to test it, thank God, so it was never confirmed as such.

Now we were getting somewhere. We were going to use the rifle grenade which entailed fitting a metal cup on the end of a .303 Enfield and putting a balacite cartridge into the breech. You then knelt on your left foot with your right knee, pointing the rifle in the direction where you wanted the grenade to land and flicking the trigger with the finger.

The Regular sergeant showed us by demonstrating the first launching. There was a sharp crack and the grenade soared to a height of about a hundred feet and with a whistle landed in the corner of the sportsfield where we were training. One of the officers wanted to be next and, obviously shaking at the knees, but bravely taking aim, he flicked the trigger. At the same time he slipped off his left foot and the grenade angled off to the left and landed on the roof of a nearby house. I say landed. It went through the roof, but fortunately as they were practice grenades and didn't explode damage was restricted. Nevertheless, we made headlines that next day.

Bill Hall
SHAFTESBURY, DORSET

As our training continued we did weekend courses, had exercises with the Regular Army, did live grenade throwing, house clearing and went on assault courses. We also went on survival courses, one of which I remember well...

On Saturday afternoon we were taken in a closed-in cattle truck and dropped in the middle of Wellsyke Wood. We were told we would be picked up again on Sunday afternoon. We had no food with us, but rabbits were plentiful and there happened to be a field of potatoes nearby and as we were all countrymen it was no problem to catch a rabbit or two. We soon had broth and stew on the menu so we proved we could be self-supporting if needs be.

Another exercise I shall always remember was going to the local RAF Station for gas drill. We all had to line up at the gas chamber door and we were told we were to run through the chamber and out a

door at the far end, but when we reached the other end the door was held for a few seconds before we were allowed out. We knew then that the gas mask was a vital piece of equipment.

As time went on I was promoted to lieutenant and given command of a platoon about five miles from company HQ. This meant I spent more of my time with men other than those I had been trained with, but I soon found that they all had the same purpose in mind, to help defend their homes and families if the need arose.

Wilfred Hodgson
CONINGSBY, LINCOLN

One incident I always remember was a party of us were detailed with a sergeant in charge to dig a communication trench, from a pill box to wherever. Two or three of us who were a lot younger than the others started to dig as though there was no tomorrow, when the sergeant in charge saw us and ordered us to stop, explained the army had a drill for digging and then proceeded to demonstrate. First movement, then a pause to the count of two, three. Second movement, pause two, three and so on until the operation of digging one spade full of earth had been completed. No doubt this drill for digging was appropriate to soldiers of the 1914–18 war with the amount of digging that was needed for trench warfare. But in 1943–44 when I was taking an active part in the Italian campaign, especially when shelled by enemy artillery, it was a case of digging a slit trench as fast and as deep as possible in the shortest possible time. I often smiled to myself when I thought of that old Home Guard sergeant and his demonstration.

Most evenings members of the Home Guard would report to the drill hall for foot or arms drill and lectures, with fatigue parties cleaning ammunition, counting ammunition, checking stores, filling sandbags when required and any other job that needed attention. Occasionally on a Sunday, that being the only day most of the Home Guard members had off from work, we would be detailed to report at Pakefield rifle range for target practice. Some of the old soldiers from the 1914–18 war were the best shots, hitting the bull's eye every time. Although being a serious exercise it was a good day out if the weather was fine, with everybody enjoying themselves.

Kenneth Horn
LOWESTOFT, SUFFOLK

We next tried our skill at grenade throwing. Of course we were throwing with a dummy grenade which was painted white, and we could do anything when throwing it. No fear in us pitching and lobbing at the enemy without a miss. However, one Sunday morning my pal and I reported for duty and in the yard were two army trucks. I remember I remarked to my mate, 'Another exercise by the look of it.' Well, we took off in the trucks and ended up in some disused ground. The lookouts were already posted and there was a deep dug-out with sandbags around it to a height of about five feet, and suddenly it dawned on us. My mate said, 'Christ, it's live grenade practice,' and I can tell you we both broke out in a cold sweat.

At last my turn came. I went down into the pit to the sergeant on duty and he handed me the grenade and I held it as if it was red hot and nearly dropped it there and then. I could see the contempt on his face. 'Hold it,' he said, 'it won't bite you.'

Then he showed me how to use it, holding it for the throw and then how to remove the pin before throwing the grenade over the top of the sandbags. The sweat was pouring down my face and how I longed for one of those old dummies even if it didn't really kill Germans.

'Pull the pin,' he said tersely. I pulled the pin and was trembling so much it's a wonder I didn't drop it there

and then in the dug-out. 'Throw,' he called and I lobbed the grenade over the top and as soon as I let it go I dived to the bottom of the dug-out.

The sergeant shouted contemptuously, 'It won't bloody hurt you.'

'Won't it?' I said. 'I've only dropped it over the other side.'

Well, whether he was a hero or as frightened as me I'll never know, but as quick as a flash he was down on top of me and then the grenade exploded and I'm not ashamed to say that from then onwards whenever it was possible I avoided grenade practice unless they were dummies.

Joe James
CWMBRAN, GWENT

Another story is what I would call the longest walk. After a lot of practice throwing dummy Mills Bombs, we were told we were to throw a live one each on Sunday morning. The military had made us a throwing range on the side of a golf link. This consisted of three adjoining semi-circular bays with a wall behind which was made of sandbags. The left bay was the assembly bay for the men. The centre was the priming bay where, under the control of a sergeant, the live grenade had a detonator inserted. The right-hand bay was the throwing bay, again with a sergeant in charge. I had to stand behind the wall at the back and observe where the bomb landed, in case it failed to explode, and then duck down. This, with a four-second fuse, was safer than it would seem.

As I was by now in charge of the platoon, I called a parade on Saturday evening in the village hall. Here we made a mock-up of the three bays, using some of the numerous chairs. We spent the entire evening practising with our dummies, all but the actual throwing. My big fear was that a trainee, in his nervousness, might drop the grenade before he was able to throw it over the top. So as each man was ready to throw I would shout, 'He's dropped it!' The sergeant then had four seconds to hustle the trainee out of the bay and round the back of the wall. We practised this over and over again.

They were no more bored than I was. We did, however, make sure we finished in time for a casual visit to the Manx Arms.

The following morning we went to the range and several grenades were thrown without incident. Then what I had dreaded happened. The trainee did not drop the grenade, but in his nervousness held on to it for too long. The grenade struck one of the top sandbags and rolled back into the bay. Instinctively I yelled, 'He's dropped it!' and crouched down pretty smartly behind the wall. There was a terrific explosion, a whine of shrapnel, and to my horror, in a cloud of dust and smoke, I saw several pieces of cloth.

I thought that the two men had been blown to pieces. Just then I heard a voice, 'You all right, sir?' There alongside me was the sergeant and the man. All the boring training had borne fruit. Instinctively on hearing the warning, the sergeant had hustled the trainee round the corner and undoubtedly saved their lives. The cloth that I had seen was, in fact, part of the sandbags.

The reason the officer in charge had to see where the grenade landed was in case it failed to explode. This, in fact, only happened to me once. The grenade has a four-second fuse. The officer had to wait under cover for five minutes and then take his helmet off. This was in case it fell off on to the grenade whilst he was stooping over it. A small explosive charge had to be assembled. This consisted of the explosive, a detonator and a length of fuse. This was placed as near as possible to the grenade without touching it.

My dud grenade was balanced on a clump of heather. I placed the charge very gingerly I may say and lit the fuse. The worst part was still to come. You had to walk back and not run. This was supposed to be so that you did not trip and fall. It seemed to me to be the longest walk I had ever taken. It was, of course, quite safe. The fuse gave you ample time to take cover. It just didn't seem like it.

W. Lockington Marshall
BALDRINE, ISLE OF MAN

The only occasion when Sergeant Metcalfe was not on top of his job was when some new weapon was allocated to the company and we had to dismantle, assemble, name the parts and 'go through the motions' of firing it. He struggled against the queries of the engineers in the unit, some of whom suggested better and quicker ways of assembling it, and others who even sketched more efficient designs. In the end, he had to resort to shouting that the method he was teaching them was the one 'in the bloody book' and if they did not shut up he would have to put them on a 'fizzer', a not very serious threat. But they knew when they had gone too far and stopped pulling his leg.

There used to be a disused quarry or out-worked chalk pit on Dunstable Downs. It was ideal for practising throwing hand grenades because an earthwork near the top could be used as a trench for throwing the grenades and taking cover. The Vauxhall Home Guard went there for practice. Major Brett was in the trench throughout the exercise and each Home Guard, as his turn came, jumped down with two grenades each. Major Brett gave the orders by numbers. One, 'prepare to throw'; two, 'pull the pin'; three, 'throw'; four, 'take cover until the explosion', he quietly commanded.

I had pulled the pin from the first grenade and was about to hurl it as far as I could when he ordered, 'Stop!'

I stopped with the pinless grenade in my hand.

'Where's the other grenade?' he asked.

'In the breast pocket of my uniform,' I replied and I pointed to the bulge with my free hand.

'Three, throw!' he yelled.

After the exercise he made a point of apologising for his hazardous intervention. But he went off enthusiastically to take pot shots at unexploded grenades with a rifle. I feel now that if anyone enjoyed the Home Guard it was Major Brett.

Peter Cane Vigor
LUTON, BEDFORDSHIRE

As time went by we developed from Fred Karno's Army into a smart fighting force with full army uniform and .303 rifles and bayonets. We had a fine commander, a Captain Kitchener, and he arranged a special parade one day through the centre of town to impress everybody. We were there to defend them. He felt very proud that day as 1,000 men of the Home Guard marched down the main street with rifles at the slope and fixed bayonets and all the town turned out that day to cheer us on.

Robert A. Eland
SCARBOROUGH, YORKSHIRE

In 1941 I was moved to Stakeford, some distance to the south, where I joined the local unit immediately. My first impression was that the unit was much more professional than the one I had just left. The men were mostly miners and the commanding officer was Lieutenant Ned Jordan, a First War veteran. Another First War survivor was

Sergeant Bates, M.M., sharing rank with Sergeant Jackie Pringle, a young dental mechanic. There was a singular lack of 'bull', with Ned Jordan and Bill Bates models of geniality – a trait which did not prevent those excellent soldiers from passing on their considerable knowledge.

Jackie Pringle, an Alan Ladd 'lookalike', soon established himself as an outstanding leader, and many and devious were the ways he devised to make training both interesting and instructive. He once hacksawed a 36 Mills hand grenade in half to show us what it looked like inside.

I worked a rota of five different shifts looking after the underground machinery at Ashington Colliery. This enabled me to go one gloriously fine Monday to a bomb throwing exercise at the nearby Barrington Brickworks.

The target was some 30 yards distant, the object being to lob grenades from behind a shallow trench with a parapet of sandbags as protection. In order to gain the correct elevation a line was stretched between two posts and the grenades had to clear the line. When the safety pin was withdrawn and the bomb was lobbed towards the target, the fuse was ignited, giving us seven seconds to grovel beneath the grass. The detonation wasn't too fearsome but the bomb case, segmented like a chocolate bar, sped over our heads in menacing fashion, with the base plug carving the air with its own hideous squeal.

The officer in charge was a youthful-looking Regular Army 'two pipper' with a spanking new uniform and a BBC Home Service accent. One could imagine him stamped with the previous day's date and 'Approved War Office'. He did not get our seal of approval. It so happened that one of the two centre throwers was left-handed and should have occupied the extreme left position. On the order to throw the outer bombs landed on target, but the two inner ones rose almost vertically, clonked together at the apex of flight, and fell plumb on top of the sandbags, only inches from us. Oh calamity.

We all looked in frozen horror as the bombs wobbled perversely, first one way then the other, the smoking fuses eating the seven seconds away. However, someone must have decided we were too young to die and the grenades dropped neatly on the other side, to explode at once. That was the day we said, 'Thank heaven, not for little girls, but for well-packed sandbags.'

Tommy Wilkinson
ASHINGTON, NORTHUMBERLAND

The arrival of the Canadian Army in the district caused quite a stir. They were far better paid than the British Army or the local farmworkers, and were very generous in buying drinks and handing out cigarettes in the local pubs. As all the signposts had been removed as an invasion precaution, the Home Guard in our area was often called out to act as guides to Canadian drivers when joint exercises took place.

Bob McGill
WEST HADDON, NORTHAMPTONSHIRE

From early 1944 to D-Day we spent a lot of nights helping the USA forces, namely the 82nd Airborne Division which was stationed near Leicester, and the American Rangers, the equivalent of our Commandos.

We would defend the objectives and they had to attack under cover of darkness. I now know that this was rehearsals for D-Day itself. But the Americans didn't take the exercises very seriously. They would walk up and practically give themselves up and then find somewhere to sleep the night away until their transport picked them up in the mornings. Perhaps they were no different to soldiers worldwide whose motto 'Sleep whenever you can' is very true. I know it was true in my case when I was eventually called up to the army.

Albert Squires
BLACKPOOL, LANCASHIRE

One parade I remember was through Newcastle. I think it was in War Weapons Week, one of the regular parades we had, and it was a very big one. Many men from each unit were picked to take part and I was one of them. We arrived at the marshalling point by way of the tramcar system. All was turmoil as all kinds of people were taking part representing all the services, civilian and military, even mobile anti-aircraft guns. We were a large contingent and were placed next to a unit of Northumberland Fusiliers. Our destination was St James' Park football ground. Any modern viewer of *Dad's Army* would have been surprised, expecting to see a shambles of old men. But what they would have seen was a large body of Home Guards with rifles at the slope in tune with the bands. Our bearing and our smartness brought special applause from the crowds. It even prompted one man to run from the crowd and he shouted to the nearby spectators, 'What do you think of "Old Bill" now then?'

Joseph O'Keefe
DUNSTON, GATESHEAD

PART III

Reserved Occupations

'Major Brett also saw to the erection of display
boards throughout the factory bearing the slogan
"It All Depends On Me" in foot-high letters.'

PETER CANE VIGOR, LUTON, BEDFORDSHIRE

Soon after World War Two began, every man over 18 years of age had to register and later be medically examined to ascertain if he was fit to be called up for service later. There were, however, many occupations considered vital to the war effort: These were classified as 'reserved occupations'. As the war dragged on many of these 'reserved occupations' were declassified, so one was always liable to be called up. I duly took my medical and was passed Grade 1. At that time I was not in a reserved occupation – this was in June, 1940. Later in the year my call-up papers arrived, telling me to report to the headquarters of the Shropshire Light Infantry at Church Stretton in Shropshire. But when I told the manager of the fabric factory that I had received my papers, he got on to the authorities claiming that as I was a 'Technical Dyer' I was exempt. This claim was accepted by the army, to my great surprise, as we were not engaged in any sort of war work.

So I returned my papers and heard no more about it. That, surprisingly, was the last I heard. With my wife's consent, I attempted later to volunteer as I felt I was cheating, but each time as soon as I mentioned my occupation and they checked in The Book, they refused my application. Telling them that I was doing nothing to help the war effort, apart from being in charge of the Fire-watching and ARP at the factory, made not the slightest bit of difference. To the service mentality what The Book said was sacrosanct.

I was always very keen to join the Home Guard and when our factory was largely taken over by another firm to produce ammunition cases, my job in ARP was ended. I then felt free to join up and so on 23 January 1941, I went along to the nearest unit of the Home Guard and was duly enrolled as a private in the Yiewsley Platoon of 'T' Sector of the London District Home Guard. The regiment was my own County Regiment, the Middlesex (The Diehards), and I was glad, for my eldest brother had been a member of the same Regiment for 20 years from 1917 to 1937.

James Frewin
SHERBORNE, DORSET

I was a member of the Home Guard from the days when it was the Local Defence Volunteers to the time when we were 'stood down'. I worked in Crewe Railway Works so I had to patrol and so called 'guard' the works. Believe me it was not like *Dad's Army*.

When we were given our uniforms and kit the last thing that we got was our greatcoats and we were very glad because the winter that year was very cold. The only difference between our kit and the Regulars was that we had leather belts and gaiters. The gaiters were too tall and so everybody that I knew had a few inches cut off them and the straps and buckles moved. Our company was attached

to the 7th Battalion Cheshire Regiment and came under orders from Chester.

We had to work all day to 5.30 p.m. and then report for guard to the works at 10 p.m. We then finished guard at 6 a.m. and for that day worked until 2 p.m. in the afternoon. At weekends we had rifle and sten gun training on the range, which was a natural amphitheatre by the River Dane.

Some chaps could not close their left eyes so I remember that many a time your target was hit before you had even fired. In the end they had to use eye patches.

We had to patrol around the workshops and telephone in from certain points. The dinner hour on nights was from 12 midnight to 2 a.m. and everybody had to work a 12-hour shift, seven days a week, one weekend off a month.

Many girls worked in the works especially in the machine shop outside where there were deep shelters. We used to be delighted if we got the 12 midnight to 2 a.m. patrol because we used to fix bayonets and then get the couples out of the shelters.

Leslie Owen Allen
CREWE, CHESHIRE

In September 1939 when the war started, I was 19 years old and ripe for the Armed Forces. However, being an electrician working on factory maintenance in the industrial area of Huddersfield, I was in a reserved occupation and, for the time being, not liable to conscription. Although tempted to volunteer for a searchlight unit, I resisted, as my father, a veteran of the First World War, had instilled in to me from childhood: 'Keep out o' t'army, nivver volunteer for nowt.'

Eric Wall
LETCHWORTH, HERTFORDSHIRE

I was a coalminer at Stanley Colliery, and as a result of not being called up I was made to join the Home Guard at Chadderden. One memory stands out a mile.

A chap named Arthur Dilley and I were in Section B. He was a top-class walker and worked in a foundry where the floors were very hot. We were lined up for inspection one evening by a Lieutenant. He looked down at Arthur's feet and said, 'Where are your issue boots?'

The reply that Arthur gave was, 'I can't wear them, sir.'

The Lieutenant sent him back home to get them but I didn't see him come back. In fact I didn't see him for five weeks. When I did he said he had been in prison for refusing to wear the boots. One month's jail. He still refused to wear them at the next parade and this time he got two months in jail.

About two years later I met him again and he said that he had done another three months in jail. Then he told me how they sent him in the army up to Scotland where they were all lined up for inspection and the first thing that the sergeant major shouted at him was, 'Now then, Dilley, forget the Home Guard.' As though I could forget that, he said.

Does anyone know of anyone else who got six months' jail for serving in the Home Guard? Not a bit like *Dad's Army*.

Dick Daniel
CHADDERDEN, DERBY

The TV series, *Dad's Army*, is certainly correct in all aspects of Home Guard activities in the first couple of years of their existence.

In Oldbury the larger firms had their own companies. The battalion was the 8th Worcesters. The town company was A Company and the works groups were B–C Companies, etc., descending in order of importance or size.

Because it was not acceptable for directors to be ordered about by workmen when on duty, they automatically became officers, despite the fact that some of the workmen were far more qualified to lead.

It therefore became quite a shambles to start with, with officers just like Captain Mainwaring in *Dad's Army*. It took the influx of Regular Army officers to get things more organised.

Incidents that come to mind are humorous and would have been tragic if it had become necessary to fight, although I had no doubt that everyone would have given his best.

We had to do night duty one evening per week and guard the headquarters or open spaces around the town. The works companies guarded their own works. In the town was Albrights & Wilson chemical manufacturers, the Midland Tar Distilleries, who produce benzine petrol as well as many other inflammable substances, so if these had been hit with a bomb during an air raid, considerable damage would have been done to the community. Luckily there were no direct hits on these works.

Eric Gregory
TAMWORTH, STAFFORDSHIRE

Our employers were very good. They never deducted anything off our pay, even though we lost two days' work. We also got a small allowance from the military. We had to fill in a form and get the captain, who was now promoted to major, to sign it before submitting it for payment.

When I said employers were good about pay I meant in the unusual cases of absence the pay was made up but the normal weekly duty was done without any time off. It was straight from night guard duty, a quick wash and change, and off to work. This was normal for fire-watchers, etc., as well as the Home Guard.

John H. Scoby
REDCAR, CLEVELAND

I joined the Home Guard in 1941 mainly because the other Voluntary Services (Civil Defence, Fire-watching, the Auxiliary Fire Service, First Aid) seemed to spend most of their training listening to lectures indoors. I was already browned off with long hours of work under artificial light on a training scheme in Vauxhall Motors Apprentice School.

Although a volunteer, I was not a very good Home Guard. I hated regimentation and communal living but the duties were not too onerous. Once a week we had to spend a 'duty' in the showrooms at Vauxhall. The early part of the evening was taken up by drilling and talks and demonstrations with the few arms we were at first issued with. Then we took turns guarding the railway bridges against saboteurs, and the factory itself from enemy parachutists bent on mischief, and the townsfolk from an invading army. We slept fitfully on camp beds, still wearing our uniforms, for about four hours a night. In any case, the cloth of the uniform became oily as I had to wear it to work during the day. I became overheated when wearing it, with the result that I contracted some form of dermatitis in the knee and elbow joints.

I had previously joined the company's Civil Defence unit (or Air Raid Precautions) because the training necessary allowed me to have an evening's respite from overtime each week, the loss of income being made up from the company who paid ARP members a shilling or two for each time they turned out – as well as providing one of those huge chunks of bread and dripping and pint mugs of tea.

Volunteers had to accomplish (wearing gas masks), various exercises, listen to boring lectures from humourless instructors, use stirrup pumps to neutralise imaginary incendiary bombs and, later in the training, extract dummy casualties from bombed buildings, the latter exercise being organised in special weekend sessions. To me the Home Guard seemed a more positive, active and, if necessary, aggressive organisation: so I joined up. This is not to denigrate the Civil Defence Services but were my thoughts at the time.

In effect, Vauxhall Motors had its own private army,

although its official designation was J Company, Beds and Herts Regiment, Home Guard. At its inauguration, the commanding officer was Major J. H. 'Bertie' Brett, whose job at Vauxhall was then an assistant to the managing director, Sir (then Mr) Charles Bartlett. There were several assistants to the managing director in the war years, whose functions few people in the factory could define. Some were senior executives whose peacetime jobs in the organisation were no longer required or whose activities had been scaled down. They were given important-sounding assignments of one kind or another.

Major Brett was responsible for installing a tannoy system for relaying air raid warnings, as the Luton sirens could not be heard above the noise of the machines. He also arranged loudspeakers which used to relay much distorted (and thereby abused by the employees) 'Music While You Work' programmes throughout the entire factory until some of the office workers objected. These BBC-

inspired programmes became unacceptable because of the type of music broadcast. Marches incited the workers to stride up and down the gangways in military fashion; dance tunes, especially in areas employing girls, made them jig about and try a few Fred Astaire steps, and vocals which seemed to make them want to howl in a hideous counterpoint.

Major Brett installed the company's own variety of 'Music While You Work' so that innocuous records of light orchestral music could be relayed and these were supposed to help production rather than distracting from it.

The day-to-day running of this programme was the responsibility of Richard McEvoy, a long-serving officer in the St John Ambulance Brigade, and a kind of sergeant-major instructor in the company's Civil Defence activities. Major Brett also saw to the erection of display boards throughout the factory bearing the slogan 'It All Depends On Me' in foot-high letters. He saw to their replacement if they were damaged or torn down accidentally. Major Brett was promoted during the latter part of the war to Lieutenant Colonel and assumed wider responsibilities in the Home Guard in Bedfordshire and Hertfordshire.

Captain K. T. Smith was promoted major. In his ordinary working life Ken Smith was then Assistant General Secretary of the Recreation Club and among his officers was Lieutenant Arthur 'Spam' Adams,

Canteen Manager, so on exercise and on training evenings the Vauxhall Home Guard was well provided with rations.

The sergeant of my platoon was Harry Metcalfe, a former Regular soldier. He was a loyal Englishman, a good Home Guard and a strict disciplinarian. Discipline was difficult to enforce in this voluntary organisation, especially when most of the men had other duties to honour, towards their work, their domestic circumstances and obligations towards street fire-watching, etc. Sergeant Metcalfe drilled us meticulously, both with arms and without, and led us on exercises into the surrounding countryside.

Weapons were in short supply in the first years of the Home Guard, broom sticks being used in rifle drill, for instance, but Major Brett, through his contacts at the War Office (Vauxhall produced army trucks, tanks, etc.), had no difficulty in providing us with .303 Enfield rifles, uniforms, and other equipment. Soon we had Tommy sub-machine guns and Lewis machine guns and a home-made Spigot Mortar which lobbed hand grenades a hundred yards or so. Major Brett even contrived to borrow a Churchill tank – they being the type built by the company – and confounded a Regular Army company in an exercise designed to take over the factory. This caused a great deal of annoyance to the commanding officer of the attacking force, as it was not considered fair for the amateur Home Guard to defeat a fully armed professional unit, so the referees decided the battle was a draw.

Most of us took Vauxhall Home Guard activities deadly seriously but there were humorous incidents in plenty. Sergeant Metcalfe enjoyed taking us out over the hills at the back of Vauxhall in reconnoitre expeditions, when with faces blackened and with twigs in our tin helmets, we crawled through hedges and across fields in the manner of proper infantrymen.

One day, however, we were amused to see Corporal Dibsdall arriving on horse-back; probably another unique event for Vauxhall Home Guard for there could not have been many cavalry Home Guard units in the country. Corporal Dibsdall, to underline his eccentricity and adventurousness, also rode his horse to work, hobbling it in one of the car parks. This was another of those occasions when the news of this event travelled all over the factory and crowds of people went to have a look, as if they had never seen a horse before.

There were about 20 camp beds in the showrooms at Vauxhall, each supplied with two stinking blankets, for they were used night after night by different people. We were expected to work all day and get about three or four hours of restless sleep at night after spending the other part of the night on duty, drilling or patrolling the factory. Then we had to get to work at 7.30 a.m. Most of my comrades slept in their uniforms to save time when called out. I could not sleep and most duty nights were a torment to me. The thought of sleeping rough or in a tent with five or six others – all probably beer drinkers – made me opt out as often as I could. I was glad for this reason alone that the war ended, but for all that, I would have endured whatever fate had in store for me had I been called to the Colours. And I would have adapted as best I could like so many others.

Peter Cane Vigor
LUTON, BEDFORDSHIRE

PART IV

Air Raids and the ARP

'We stood outside watching from time to time flames roaring across the sky and it was only then that we started to find out about the V1 flying bombs, which were called "Doodlebugs". Someone said, "Have you noticed that when the noise stops and the flames cut out it's followed shortly afterwards by an explosion?" So we watched and we noticed that they were right. Little did we know what they were until we were told the next morning.'

FRANK TAYLOR, ROMFORD, ESSEX

At the outbreak of war I was a member of St John's Church, Boys Brigade, and all members over the age of 16 were asked if they would like to volunteer for civil defence work, acting as messengers to the Report Centre at Lowestoft Police Station, Regent Road. Several of us volunteered, staying as messengers, until being called up for military service.

After the outbreak of war, Lowestoft took on a different role, changing from a fishing port to a naval base, with most of the fishing boats being converted to mine sweepers and patrol vessels. At the time most of the crews were in the Royal Navy Reserve and were called up almost immediately for service in the Navy.

Apart from men being called up for military service and the organisation of civil defence workers taking duties such as special constables, air raid wardens, fire services, first aid and ambulance crews, also heavy and light rescue teams, life went on about the same as normal, with little or no signs of enemy activity until June 1940 when Lowestoft had its first air raid. I was on my way to report for duty at the Report Centre and as I was cycling along Milton Road, past Granville Road, I heard a burst of machine gun fire from aircraft flying overhead. A few yards further on as I crossed Clapham Road, I looked up and saw bombs dropping, the first one exploding on the right side of Clapham Road, the others falling on to the Co-op shops on the opposite side of the road, causing considerable damage. On reaching the Report Centre I reported what I had seen, when at that moment another messenger arrived, confirming my story. He was employed in the office at the Co-op and said all the staff had managed to get to the shelters in time and there were no casualties.

After the first air raid, bombing raids became more frequent. During one on a Saturday evening, a bomb dropped, exploding on the corner of Regent Road and Police Station Road, causing some damage to the Report Centre. Hearing the bomb whistling down we dived for cover under a large leather-topped table. After the bomb exploded we went to the control room next door, to see if everybody was okay. When we saw each other we burst out laughing. It was only then that we noticed what a mess we were, covered in soot, plaster and dust. At least it eased the tension.

Some time later, during another air raid, a bomb exploded almost on the same spot as before, at the corner of Regent Road and Police Station Road. On this occasion, however, the damage was much worse, forcing the Report Centre to move, taking temporary accommodation in Church Road Junior School (now demolished),

until a more suitable and specially designed Report Centre was built. When it was finally completed the Report Centre moved into its new premises, towards the end of 1941. About this time a letter from one of the Government Ministries arrived at the Report Centre with an attached list showing the worst bombed places in the country, with Plymouth and Coventry heading the list, Lowestoft fifth and London in ninth or tenth place. It was based on the area covered by the city or town and numbers of population. At the same time it was decided that all voluntary civil defence workers would be paid. Messengers to receive 3d per hour.

One Wednesday evening at approximately 9.30 p.m. German bombers flew over the town, dropping hundreds of incendiary bombs and starting several large fires. Woolworths store in London Road North, Austin & Wales Wholesale Grocery, a garage, a billiard hall, two dance halls and several small cottages in the Clapham Road and Raglan Street area, plus the railway goods depot being the worst hit with several smaller fires. The Fire Services were stretched to the limit on this occasion. At the same time other bombers were dropping high explosive bombs causing further damage.

The following Monday night German bombers tried the same tactics at Pakefield. After incendiary bombs had set fire to the roof of Pakefield Parish Church, a thick fog came down putting a stop to any further bombing that night.

Mr Kenneth Horn
LOWESTOFT, SUFFOLK

When I was nearly 14 I joined the ARP as a Fire Guard Messenger. It was only because the headquarters had a snooker table and I was learning the game. I had to report for duty with my bicycle all clean and shiny.

All went well until one Sunday during an exercise when I was sent with a message to the next ARP Post about a mile away. Unfortunately I got lost and I couldn't find the Post and by the time I had returned to our Post the whole exercise had finished. So not knowing what to do I went round to the chief ARP Warden of our Post to tell him and promptly burst into tears when all he did was roll about laughing.

Clifford B. Fawcett
NELSON, LANCASHIRE

During the Battle of Britain we were being heavily bombed at Portland during the daylight raid and Crown Farm at Easton received a direct hit. My grandfather's house was almost directly opposite the farm, and was at that time occupied by my aunt and her daughter. My father was an ARP warden.

After the raid my aunt sent her daughter to our house saying, 'Please come quickly, Uncle Ned, there's a German parachutist in the attic, we can hear his gun going off.'

My father put on his 'tin hat' and set off immediately to grandfather's house. Sure enough when he arrived he could hear the bangs quite clearly.

In fear and trepidation he mounted the steps to the attic but could see no one in the darkness. But he could hear the bangs all right. Investigating further he found, stored between the roof slates and the rafters, bottles of brandy whose corks were popping owing to the vibration caused by the bomb explosion. The brandy must have been hidden there by my grandmother who had at that time been dead for nearly 40 years. Many people of Portland were engaged in

smuggling in the old days and there appears to be no doubt at all that the brandy was in fact contraband and goodness knows how old.

My father 'rescued' what bottles he could find, and handed these down the attic steps to my aunt.

However, she was a staunch 'Salvationist' and she promptly poured them down the drain each time he passed them down to her without him knowing it whilst he was going back up into the attic. Her comment was: 'I would never be able to hold my head up again in the Army if I knew such liquor was under my roof.'

My father eventually managed to 'escape' with a bottle of brandy in each pocket, purely for medicinal purposes you understand. And so that was the saga of the illicit 'brandy run'.

Mrs Evelyn Hodder
WAREHAM, DORSET

Nowadays no one seems to have heard of the Cyclist Messenger Corps but it was just as much a part of the civilian support for the Armed Services as the Home Guard. I don't know who was the originator of it but I believe it was someone in the Boy Scouts Association and certainly all the ones in the Nottingham area seemed to be scouts.

I belonged to the 98th Nottingham (St Christopher's) Scout Group, and everyone in that Troop not in the Armed Forces volunteered for the ARP Cyclist Messenger Corps. Every time the sirens went we had to report to our warden post or 'Incident Officer'. Our job was to carry messages to headquarters or anywhere else if the phone wires were down. I remember that my brother Roy was in the Corps and that one day when he was shot at by a passing aircraft he was most indignant because it was his birthday. He was a headquarters Messenger and as Nottingham ARP headquarters was at 'Eastcroft', London Road and my brother worked in Boots Publicity Department on Parkinson Street (only five minutes' walk away) he was given permission to leave work and report to his post. I was also in full time employment in Nottingham but only reported for night air raid warnings. It is only in later years that one realises just how much one's parents must have worried.

In my mind I can still hear the internal loudspeaker system which broadcast once a month:

YOU ARE NOW GOING TO HEAR THE DANGER IMMINENT SIGNAL. IF YOU HEAR THIS SIGNAL AT ANY OTHER TIME, GO AT ONCE TO YOUR SHELTER OR DUTY POST. THIS IS A TEST ONLY.

Then followed an ear splitting klaxon blast in short one-second blasts with a short pause in between. We used to cover our ears with both hands and I used to shout, 'Oh, shut up!' The klaxon of course was so loud that no one could hear me shouting. Unfortunately one day I mistimed the noise and was still shouting at the top of my voice when the klaxon abruptly stopped. I got a 'Have you gone quite crazy Dennis?' from my boss.

Although I was only 16 I was also the department Fire Warden and had been trained by Boots Fire Brigade to use a stirrup pump and also a full size fire hose. We had to crawl into a metal shed and put out a large blazing fire with a stirrup pump and a bucket of water. I quite enjoyed squirting water in the canal with the fire hose.

If the danger warning sounded I had to make sure that everyone had gone to the basement shelters, checking right around the Department including the men's and ladies' toilets. Only then could I dash down the emergency stairs which led directly to the air raid shelters.

Apart from the two main staircases at each end of the department there were two emergency staircases. On the first Monday of every month I had to check both these staircases to make sure they were not obstructed in any way. I used to put the crash-bar of one door on its hook then run down one set of stairs and up the other. I often used to time myself to see if I could do it in record time. One day I was hurtling down the stairs and crashed into a young couple who were snogging on the staircase. I knew both of them and can even remember the girl's name. I of course did not report them as they would have undoubtedly both have got the sack.

Dennis H. Brooks
BURTON JOYCE, NOTTINGHAM

During an air raid several bombs and incendiaries landed in the centre of Oldbury town. I was on duty that particular night and we had to help in putting out the fire. Incendiary bombs that landed in the road were covered with a sandbag and left to burn out. We followed the trail of the incendiaries across some back streets using a stirrup pump to put them out and the small fires they started. If you got them before a big blaze developed you could handle the situation, otherwise you called the Fire Brigade if it got out of hand.

During this sortie chasing the small incendiaries, we found one that had fallen through an outdoor coalhouse roof and was sitting on top of the coal getting a nice fire going. We found that the coalhouse door was padlocked so we banged on the back door to get the owner to open up. We got no answer so we smashed the padlock off with the butt of a rifle. While we were doing this a back window opened and a voice roared out, 'Stop it, you thieving buggers.' This man had slept through an air raid, the banging on his door, but as soon as someone touched the padlock it woke him up.

Eric Gregory
TAMWORTH, STAFFORDSHIRE

Air activity had increased over the South Wales district and on a Thursday winter's evening 22 January 1941 I was in a tram car entering town to participate in my Home Guard duties. Queen Street (the main street in Cardiff) was suddenly showered with incendiaries, which like sparklers were bursting all along the street. The tram stopped, everyone had to get off and the air raid siren started to wail. There now sounded the cracking of anti-aircraft guns, more incendiaries and now the strong unsynchronised throbbing of the aircraft.

Making my way toward the C.W.S. emporium where I worked, I saw the windows were blown out and another shower of incendiaries landed. Accompanied by other members of the Home Guard company we entered the emporium and went upstairs four floors and on to the roof.

Playing the stirrup pumps on to the bombs and picking up any we could with special tongs for this purpose, we threw most over into the street below – earning the displeasure of some irate ARP wardens below. Those lodged in the rafters we examined as closely as we could and either pushed through or pulled out before carting them over to a strong corner of the roof and placing sandbags on them. Apparently what we didn't know was that certain incendiaries with a black band exploded after a period to injure likely idiots like us if we got too close. Fortunately nobody was injured. We succeeded in putting out all the fires in the roof but saw that Longs the Jewellers below us had two incendiaries burning in their roof, but out of reach and a long drop down. One brilliant Home Guard dropped a wet weighty sandbag directly on top of the bomb, but this also shattered the roof tiles and the whole issue disappeared into the jewellers.

Fortunately one of our Home Guard was the jeweller's manager and we rushed down the stairs and next door to the jeweller's shop. The number of locks and gates, doors, etc., which had to be opened took ages and after much effort we managed to get to the spot where the incendiaries were now spluttering and with the use of a bucket took both out of the building. During the whole time there were explosions and even the large Co-op building shuddered, when a near miss hit our HQ at the wholesale building directly opposite. I believe we were all too ignorant to be frightened. Directly or indirectly we saved the buildings and each of us received a cheque and letter of commendation.

Cardiff had received a severe raid that night and many churches and other buildings were burned out. It was not as severe as Bristol or Swansea but about 400 people were killed, Neville Street and Deburgh Street being names every Cardiff person will remember.

Bill Hall
SHAFTESBURY, DORSET

One of my tasks was despatch rider. Whenever there was a raid, our headquarters in the Queen's Regiment building in Jamaica Road, Bermondsey, had to have a list of all personnel in our building in the event of there being casualties. It was my (and others') job to get it there. It was about a mile and a half away on my bike and I wore a blue and white armband to show how important my job was. It was not uncommon to have to dodge around craters and on one occasion there was such a huge one that I had to pick up my bike and run down the crater and up the other side before I could resume my journey.

This particular night most of the Home Guard chaps were out on jobs and the diversity of jobs would amaze you. The only persons I saw were the colonel and the Adjutant calmly playing snooker. Colonel Crawford had been a Royal Flying Corps pilot in World War One and had a slightly withered arm. I asked them for their list of personnel to take back with me and he said I must wait a while as it wasn't ready. He saw how nervous I was and told me to get a cup of tea from the canteen while I waited, and I complied. However, I was so scared, because being near the docks the area was taking a real pasting, that my cup and saucer were rattling like crazy. Our very calm colonel, seeing my predicament, said for me to get under the table with my tea. Every time a bomb came near, the table jumped a few inches off the floor but that didn't ruffle our intrepid pair. They merely waited till the balls stopped jumping about and resumed play. I certainly couldn't wait to get out of there fast as I realised that if the building did get hit I would have had to cope with about two ton of billiard table on me as well.

Fred Woolford
ROMFORD, ESSEX

Oone place nobody wanted to guard was the main electrical substation situated in a small field away from the works across the main Holyhead line. It was a concrete building filled with switch gear, three army beds, no heating and a concrete floor.

In the field also was a barrage balloon manned by the RAF. Then, it seemed suddenly, the RAF men vanished and were replaced by the Women's Royal Air Force, and suddenly everybody wanted to guard the electrical substation works. We used to guard the substation as single guards at first with five rounds in the rifle, watching the searchlights probing the sky for the bombers and then converging if one was caught and I remember Ack-Ack peppering the sky with what we called 'flaming onions'.

Leslie Owen Allen
CREWE, CHESHIRE

When I joined the Home Guard I was living in my home town of Reading in Berkshire and, with several other men, some I already knew, and others who became friends, we reported to the drill hall at Yeomanry

House which was battalion headquarters for the Home Guard companies in the Reading area.

There were men from all walks of life. Many of them had seen service in the 1914–18 war. I think I was probably the youngest in this particular squad. Twice a week for the next ten weeks we were given basic training in a similar manner to the Regular Army, including a few choice words from the regimental sergeant major, a veteran of the First World War.

I think it was about four weeks later that we were issued with uniforms, gas mask, tin helmet and allocated a rifle. Most of us quite enjoyed this training and with the war situation at that time very uncertain we felt that at least we had some idea what to do had there been an invasion. At the end of basic training we were interviewed by the RCM [Regimental Corporal Major] and allowed to decide which company we would like to be attached to. As I was working on radio repairs and maintenance I chose Signals Section, which was based at Yeomanry House headquarters, known as 7BRX (7th Berks).

One night a week we did an all-night duty, mainly manning the switchboard. In the event of an air raid warning we at HQ were informed first and it was our job to telephone the other companies and issue either an air raid message BLUE, which meant enemy aircraft heading towards the country, followed by air raid message RED, full alert, enemy aircraft in the immediate area. On red alert we set up an observation post on the flat roof of

Yeomanry House so that incendiary bombs, etc., could be reported to the ARP and police. As well as night duty we attended one evening per week for lectures and instruction on field warfare, and as we were Signals Section, communication procedures were practised. Although we had walkie-talkie radios we also learnt how to send and receive messages in Morse code. After some weeks I found that I was able to do this at quite a good speed.

Cyril Bird
FRIMLEY, SURREY

O ne time I was on all night guard duty when we had a heavy air raid. We were in an old dere-

lict house on the edge of Fairlop Aerodrome. We were supposed to be a mobile patrol. We were taken from company headquarters in an old lorry with no sides. We all had to stand up and hold on to one another when it went round corners.

In the morning we all had to push it to get it started. I say again we were supposed to be a *mobile* patrol. We went on standby all night as nobody had any details about the bombing or had heard anything. They even gave us ten rounds of ammunition.

We stood outside watching from time to time flames roaring across the sky and it was only then that we started to find out about the V1 flying bombs, which were called 'Doodlebugs'. Someone said, 'Have you noticed that when the noise stops and the flames cut out it's followed shortly afterwards by an explosion?' So we watched and we noticed that they were right. Little did we know what they were until we were told the next morning.

Frank Taylor
ROMFORD, ESSEX

I belonged to the Westbourne Platoon of 'A' Company of the First Sussex Battalion Home Guard and we wore the cap badge of the Royal Sussex Regiment. I still have my cap badge and can recite the story of its origins. Our platoon commander was a lieutenant who had previously served in the Territorial Army (London Irish Rifles). The 60 men in the platoon were divided into six sections, each under a sergeant or corporal and then into three sub-sections of a lance corporal and two privates. We paraded every sixth night from 10 p.m. until 6 a.m., with additional Sunday exercises including range practice and grenade throwing.

The usual parade night routine was to assemble in the Cricketers' Arms for liquid refreshment and then proceed by cycle to our headquarters in a disused isolation hospital. Being the youngest of the section at 16 years old, I had the job of collecting the Browning automatic rifle (.300) and the haversack of ammunition from the platoon commander's house. We all had cycles. The only member of the platoon I believe who had a car was Lieutenant Rule, the commanding officer. Perhaps that's why he was an officer. On arrival at our headquarters, the first job was to light the stove and get a kettle on for tea or cocoa. Second job was to read any new orders and check our weapons. Our sergeant had been in the Royal Marines during and after World War One but was now a carter on a local farm. That is, he looked after the horses. His name was Sergeant Silvester. He taught me a lot about firearms and I can still remember some of his sayings after 50 years.

If there was no air raid in progress then one sentry stood outside the entrance with the other two men of the sub-section just inside, while the other two sub-sections got some sleep until it was their watch. During air raids one man would be sent to man the sandbagged lookout in the garden of the farm where I both lived and worked. The lookout had a crude instrument for plotting the fall of bombs, shot down aircraft, parachutists, etc. During raids, steel helmets were worn. They were very necessary during the heavy raids on Portsmouth when shrapnel literally rained down. Although the watch ended at 6 a.m., our section had permission to pack up earlier as we were nearly all farmworkers and started milking or caring for the horses at 6 a.m. During harvesting it was particularly hard to work for 12 hours or more and then stand sentry at 3 a.m. Remember in those years we had no combines or tractors, only men and horses.

Bob McGill

WEST HADDON, NORTHAMPTONSHIRE

At approximately 4 p.m. on Tuesday 13 January 1942, during a heavy snowstorm, a lone German bomber flew low over the town dropping a stick of bombs on the main shopping centre in London Road, causing considerable damage to shops and offices, killing 77 civilians and an untold number of Naval Ratings and Wrens, who were then having tea at Waller's restaurant. The numbers of Naval personnel killed were never published but one estimate was well over 100. That brought the total number of people killed to approximately 200. One of the Report Centre messengers was killed, working as a shop assistant in one of the shops demolished in this raid.

People at this time were exhausted through lack of sleep and still having to do a normal day's work the next day. In order to get a good night's sleep hundreds of people left town each night to walk to the surrounding villages for a room and a bed which the village people were only too willing to let, appreciating what the towns people had to contend with night after night. From

3 September 1939 to 8 May 1945 the war lasted five years and eight months, making a total of 2,074 days, and during the whole of that time it was claimed Lowestoft had 2,047 air raid alarms – almost one a day.

Kenneth Horn
LOWESTOFT, SUFFOLK

PART V

Defending Against the Enemy

'When [Churchill] uttered those magic words "We will defend our island, whatever the cost may be… we will never surrender", the whole place erupted. Men and girls danced a jig on the pub counter, people were laughing and slapping each other on the back in sheer joy. That man was our idol and we would have died before we let him down. Now we would show them. And we did.'

FRED WOOLFORD, ROMFORD, ESSEX

After the evacuation from Dunkirk there was a lot of talk of a German invasion and British bombers were making regular attacks on the French ports where the invasion fleet was reported to be assembling.

On Saturday 8 September 1940 at around midnight all Home Guard units in the country were alerted and ordered to report to their headquarters. The local village hall was commandeered. All members were issued with their various weapons and ammunition and ordered to man all observation and checkpoints. I was detailed to set up a checkpoint in the main street through our village and check every vehicle. At the time a well-known Scottish regiment was stationed in the village and you can imagine the state some of them were in after a night in the local pub drinking their national tipple.

We stood to all night expecting any minute to hear the sound of aircraft or to get a message to say that the enemy had landed, but nothing happened and at 0800 hours next morning we were given the order to stand down.

I mentioned observation posts were manned during the invasion scare. Well I think we had one of the best in the country, Tattershall Castle. Patrols were posted nightly at the top of the Castle. Each consisting of four men, one NCO and three other ranks. I was in charge of one such patrol and one of the men with me was a local butcher's son and as we had only straw palliasses to lay on when we were off watch, he decided he could improve the bedding situation. So he brought a large sack of unwashed sheep locks. I'm sure if any enemy had landed within half a mile of us they would have been driven back by the smell. Needless to say we were pleased to go back to the hard palliasses.

One of our main objectives while on watch at Tattershall Castle was to report any suspicious light, but the whole of the time we were there I cannot remember ever seeing any. There were of course always rumours of lights being seen at different places and one persistent rumour was that lights were often seen coming from some derelict farm buildings in Wildmoor Fen, so our company commander decided we would investigate. So myself and two more men set off on foot one bright moonlit night. When we were about half a mile from the buildings we crawled across open fields and when we were about 100 yards away the shape of a man's head and shoulders appeared in the moonlight through one of the windows. At the same time I heard the click of a rifle at the side of me and when the man was asked what he was doing he whispered, 'I'm going to give him one,' and I believe he would have done if he had not been stopped. The shape we saw in the window was our company commander who had approached the building from the opposite direction without informing the rest of the patrol.

Wilfred Hodgson
CONINGSBY, LINCOLN

On the night of 7 September 1940 my grandfather received the Red Alert from Southern Command. Enemy parachutists had been spotted and suddenly it was deadly serious. This was war for real and to signal the invasion my father went to toll the bell at St Paul's Church along the road. Since the war began all church bells throughout the land had been silenced and were only to be rung if there was an invasion. It was a strange feeling lying in bed listening to the church bell and wondering what would happen to us all now that the invasion had really begun. The atmosphere in our house was very tense that night and the telephone rang incessantly.

My mother came up to my room and told me on no account to listen to any of the strategic planning that was going on downstairs – if I was going to be interrogated by the Germans I could not lie if I knew nothing, and there must be no question of ever giving information to the enemy – so I buried my head under the bed clothes and waited. We got almost no sleep that night and by morning we learnt that it had all been a false alarm – the first of many as it turned out, although I believe that was the only time the church bells were actually rung.

Mrs Jane Uren
TENTERDEN, KENT

It must have been some time in September 1940 and I had just stepped out of our house in Armstrong Street when a Home Guard despatch rider pulled up beside me.

'Your name is O'Keefe isn't it?'

'Yes, why?' I said.

'Report to the Lecture Hall at once. The invasion has started.'

'Surely you mean a practice exercise,' I said.

'No,' he shouted. 'They've landed on the south-east coast!' and he roared off to round up the other men.

Other men may have reacted differently, but my reaction was to run into the house, tell them all that the invasion had started, and wrapping some bread in some paper and thrusting it into my pocket as I expected to be away from home for a long time.

All was chaos at the Lecture Hall. Home Guards were coming in from all over the area. They were roughly formed into groups and sent to all the strategic points in the village.

I was sent with a group to the railway bridge on Ellison Road. There used to be some waste ground there with a slight hollow in it. There we settled ourselves down to await events. We had been issued with five rounds of ammunition each, and I thought that if we didn't get some more ammunition soon it was going to be the shortest defence in history. But I'm sure if the invasion had been genuine things would still have been attended to.

The spot where we sat is now covered by an ornamental display, and a tree is planted on the exact spot. When we passed by it one day I said jokingly to the wife that the tree had been planted there by a grateful government and one day a plaque will be nailed to the tree to commemorate our defence.

Joseph O'Keefe
DUNSTON, GATESHEAD

One incident that I remember happened one Sunday morning in September 1940 just after parade. A German aircraft, possibly a Junkers 88, passed over us very low and dropped a bomb nearby. No damage was caused, but one person was killed. The aircraft turned and on its return run our commanding officer, Lieutenant D. Holton, fired several rounds at the aircraft as it passed near us. Lieutenant Holton received a certificate of gallantry for his action.

Harold G. Guest
WELLINGBOROUGH, NORTHAMPTONSHIRE

My memories of the Home Guard: Standing on top of our local glen with *a block of wood*, expecting thousands of Germans coming down from the sky. What was I going to do with it? I never knew. By the way there were two more men to help me.

Later learning to throw grenades, but fearful of forgetting to let go. I remember one of the men dropped his bomb and the sergeant had to move very quickly to pick it up and throw it. I think he deserved a medal for that.

Somebody shouting 'Halt, who goes there?' to a cow and getting a 'moo moo' as a response.

We had quite a lot of training – and I'm quite sure we would have done a very good job of defending our country.

Well, maybe.

Leonard Jackson
DUKINFIELD, CHESHIRE

When my dad was issued with his uniform he was very proud of it, having served in the First World War. He took great care of it, but we did hear stories of the overcoats being used as an extra cover on beds during the cold winters. My mum always made us sleep downstairs (on the floor, the settee or two chairs pushed together) when Dad was on duty, but we went back upstairs when he was in. I have never worked out why we were safe when he was in. I don't think his Home Guard training would have stopped a bomb hitting if it was meant for us.

About six Home Guards used to do all night duty on top of Etching Hill, which is quite a big hill on the

Mrs Vincent's dad Rowland Hill on the left

outskirts of the town. In those days you could see for many miles in the daytime, but it must have been as black as a bag up there in the blackout. So I don't really know what they were guarding.

One night in particular my dad was on duty with a few others when they heard a plane coming over. Dad said they all looked at one another and said, 'That's a Jerry.' We'd all become experts at recognising the different sounds of 'our own' and 'Jerries' by then. Then suddenly there was an almighty bang.

They all came to the conclusion very quickly that it was a bomb, and that it was in the direction of the town. They all decided immediately that they were going home to make sure their families were all right.

They had to take a lot of leg pulling for leaving their post and they also got a ticking off from their officer. In fact it turned out to be a land mine that had dropped just the other side of town. It fell in a field and in fact did very little damage although the blast from it did break a few windows in the town.

Mrs M. Vincent
RUGELEY, STAFFORDSHIRE

At that time we lived in Bovingdon in a very rural area and had a two and a quarter acre garden adjoining a farm. In one of the fields was a water tower to pump water up to the village, which stood on a high hill.

I well remember that at that time everyone was very concerned with 'Fifth Columnists'. The platoon which my husband and many of his friends joined had the task of guarding the water tower at night. All of them were veterans from the 1914–18 war, but there were always two on duty together. At first no one had any ammunition except my husband who also had his German rifle.

They made a hole through our hedge so that they could get to the water tower without going all the way to the village and crossing the farmyard. My husband was a doctor and very used to night calls so a telephone line was installed from the top of the tower to his bedroom and each night the two on duty had to report to him that they had arrived. The impression everyone had was that we should see Fifth Columnists floating down in parachutes.

For this reason his German rifle was kept loaded just inside the front door. Presumably it was to shoot them down as they descended on to our tennis court. I always said to him that if that happened we would then both have to fly out to render first aid and bring them in.

Hilda K. Burnet
HEMEL HEMPSTEAD, HERTFORDSHIRE

Unarmed combat never appealed to me, weighing as I did but nine stone wearing full kit. I felt that against some of the more sadistic members of the company who seemed to revel in throwing the rest of us all over the drill hall, we should have been allowed to use the butt ends of our rifles just to even things up a bit. The sergeant who told me that I was a match for any 12 Germans armed or unarmed must surely have been joking.

Had the worst happened and we'd been thrown into the battle against invading forces, I wonder at what stage in the proceedings we would have been allowed to take our clip of five bullets out of our greatcoat pockets, where the clip usually rested, and insert it in our rifles. It was usually the last place we were allowed to have it in most of the time. Ammunition pouches were receptacles usually for dried egg and spam sandwiches, or occasionally, very occasionally, milk chocolate covered digestive biscuits. Gas mask holders were sometimes used to carry refreshments in as well.

John Slawson
HEYWOOD, LANCASHIRE

We developed a master plan to save Grantchester. We envisaged that the Germans would either take Cambridge or bypass it. They would then do a pincer movement on Grantchester, coming from Barton on one side and Trumpington on the other. 'B', the Classics Professor, and I were given the Stokes Mortar and the task of stopping the *third* Panzer tank as it crossed the Mill Bridge. 'B' lived on the Mill Bridge, in the converted Mill of Chaucer and Rupert Brooke fame.

It had to be the third Panzer because we had worked it all out. The first Panzer was to go through and round two sharp bends. There it would meet a mine in the middle of the road. It would stop. Hidden Home Guards would trundle a mine on strings across behind

it. Then grenades and Molotov Cocktails would engulf it in flame. The second Panzer would round the first corner and meet the same fate. But the third Panzer would receive a direct hit as it crossed the bridge from our Stokes Mortar, a sort of metal drainpipe, and so prevent any other tanks from reaching the village. It was all very theoretical and probably wouldn't have worked like that at all but it was *our* plan and we believed in it.

Alan Lawrie
LUDLOW, SHROPSHIRE

We had been alerted that at any time we could be called on suddenly to 'Battle Stations' and one Saturday a corporal called at my home and instructed me to mobilise immediately, bring emergency rations, contact two other members of the platoon and report to HQ as quickly as possible.

Within a very short time I was cycling off to call on the other two, they in turn contacted others and so on till we all signed on at HQ.

It was of course just an exercise to test our speed in responding to an emergency and in the event it lasted well into Sunday and was considered to be a success, involving as it did the rest of the Reading companies.

Cyril Bird
FRIMLEY, SURREY

We had a number of weapons. A Northover Projector, which was six foot of drainpipe mounted on two legs into which was inserted a bottle of phosphorus, a wad of black powder and the breach was closed. Then you inserted a cartridge, fired and the bottle went several hundred yards and broke into flames. Half of them didn't break and then the riflemen had to waste their time shooting at them.

We had an EY rifle which was a rifle coiled with wire, and a cup fitted to the barrel. It was loaded with a ballistic cartridge. It was a .30 Mills type, and the pin was removed and placed in the cup and fired. Alas, one day a grenade was used by mistake and fitted minus the pin, and it blew up causing the deaths of an officer and two men.

Then there were 'sticky bombs'. These were a glass dome covered in a sticky substance which was encased in a metal cover. A handle was screwed in and became a detonator. You removed the metal casing, held it at arm's length, approached the tank and smashed the glass on to the tank and walked away. The bomb would then explode. I never met any man yet who walked away. They ran. It was much to the annoyance of the NCOs and officers standing at least 100 yards away, but then they were all right.

Then there was the Sten gun. It was a useful gun but it lacked a finger guard, resulting in injuries to almost everyone to the top of the little finger or even worse the loss of it. That was until 'the powers that be' decided to do something and actually fitted a guard.

R. *Tredget*
ROMFORD, ESSEX

I can remember one particular incident when the Germans were bombing Nottingham. I set off from my home at the top of Dale Grove but quickly had to abandon my bike because of puncturing both tyres on broken glass.

Narrowly missing a bomb that fell at the bottom of Dale Grove I ran like the wind down Westward Road. Windows were blowing out all around me and as I ran up Sneinton Boulevard five incendiary bombs crashed into the road completely surrounding me.

I was half blinded with the glare and more than a little frightened. I put my arms across my face and jumped through what looked like the largest gap.

Arriving at the warden post I reported to the Senior Warden that incendiaries had fallen on Sneinton Boulevard School and were burning in the gutters. One of the young Wardens, Geoff Savage, and myself were sent out to see if the school was actually on fire.

As we crossed over the railway bridge we heard a bomb coming right over our heads and it fell in front of us on the corner of Port Arthur Road. Luckily we were both unhurt, but I believe it was this bomb which killed all five members of a fire-watchers stirrup pump team.

Geoff's two sisters were both wardens, and I went with the youngest one into the vicarage to phone through to headquarters. Hearing another bomb coming down I grabbed her and the phone and dived under the vicar's desk. Luckily it was a big strong piece of furniture because all the windows promptly blew in. What an experience for a 16-year-old boy.

Dennis H. Brooks
BURTON JOYCE, NOTTINGHAM

On occasions during summer evenings in 1941, some of us would cycle up to Links Road, at the north end of North Parade, to watch the patrol boats laying at anchor a short distance from shore. At times we saw them being bombed, sometimes disappearing from view, behind a huge spout of water sent up by an exploding bomb. After the water subsided it was a relief to see the boat still there, apparently with little or no damage. Later when talking to some of the crew of the patrol boats they said what they disliked most was during the hours of darkness German 'E' boats would sometimes patrol up and down the coast, between the patrol vessels and the shore.

Mr Kenneth Horn
LOWESTOFT, SUFFOLK

One Sunday morning during the Battle of Britain there was an air battle raging overhead when I and another Home Guard member, Harry, spotted a parachute descending from an enemy plane between Wigmore and Walderslade. We jumped into Harry's car and drove at speed across the fields and closed on the airman who was a German airgunner. We took him prisoner, disarmed him and Harry decided to take his helmet and some of his equipment as souvenirs.

A few weeks later Harry received a summons from the Air Ministry for taking enemy equipment belonging to the Crown. Harry engaged the best counsel for his defence and the case was heard in the North Aylesford Magistrates Court. His counsel quoted from an apparently ancient Act of Parliament which made it legal for Harry to keep the equipment and so he was vindicated.

Several years later, as Chairman of the Local Bench, I met Harry's counsel who was by then a High Court Judge and he informed me that the case has been reported as far away as Australia.

Major Paul T. Rogers, M.B.E., J.P.
BEARSTED, MAIDSTONE, KENT

In March 1942 a typical article in the local newspaper by journalist J. Manning read as follows:

The local platoon of the Home Guard had a realistic exercise last Sunday, when it was assumed that a number of parachutists had landed with the object of sabotaging the Water Tower. It was the job of the remainder of the platoon to round the intruders up, and to take one or two prisoners for questioning. Fifth columnists came into the picture, and included a buxom young woman with rather too much face decoration, a man with a pickaxe, a stray fisherman and a gentleman interested in the lady. The necessary prisoners were taken, and the remainder were rounded up, but not without a great deal of difficulty. The 'civilians' all carried bombs and wicked-looking knives which they introduced with good effect and from which several lessons were taught. There is no doubt that if any of the Huns arrive here uninvited the local Home Guard will give a good account of itself – and not with pikes.

Albert John Freeman
MABLETHORPE, LINCOLNSHIRE

All sorts of weapons were tried out on the poor old Home Guard, some were more dangerous to you than the enemy.

One such weapon was called the Blacker Bombard. This consisted of a tube that would take a milk bottle that had been filled with a mixture of petrol and phosphorus. A small charge was first inserted in the barrel followed by the bottle which, when it struck an object, burst into flames.

The problem was that it was so unpredictable that in order to be sure of hitting anything you had to be within about ten feet of it, and then the subject had to be as big as a house. We pointed out that we did not think that the German tanks would hardly just let us get that close in order to have a chance of hitting the side of the tank with a bottle of petrol. The other problem was that if the little charge was too big it burst the bottle in the barrel and sprayed everyone in the near vicinity with flaming petrol. Needless to say this weapon did not become a firm favourite.

Eric Gregory
TAMWORTH, STAFFORDSHIRE

We had petrol bombs and we planned out the village where these nasty bottles of liquid could be dropped or thrown on to the enemy vehicles as they passed by. It could be a narrow road with woods on either side, or bridges between our local villages, or in fact anywhere. It was all quite exciting for a young teenager.

Reginald Underwood
IPSWICH, SUFFOLK

Although I can recall many humorous happenings the one that is most vivid in my memory has a more sombre note and to my knowledge is the only occasion when the 5th North Stafford Home Guard came into contact with the enemy.

At about 4 a.m. one summer morning, Major Palmer, the commander of B Company, called at my house, saying that a German plane, which had been on a bombing raid over Manchester, had landed behind the Roaches. I collected my rifle as we raced along Buxton Road to a left side lane near the Royal Cottage. Then after a short distance we turned left again down a cart track to a farm where we left the car and then over fields down a rough boulder-strewn valley.

The first indication of the disaster was a propeller and about 100 yards further there was a dead airman. Fifty yards further we came across the crashed German Junkers 88 bomber, which had crashed head first into the hillside. The front of the plane was completely burnt to a cinder and only the tail part of the fuselage which was riddled with bullet holes was recognisable. It was a horrible scene; one dead German lay sprawled across a boulder with all his clothing burnt off him, another was badly smashed up in the tail of the fuselage.

An RAF Security officer met us and said that one member of the crew was not accounted for and asked me if I would help him search the valley which descended towards Gradbach. He had a revolver and I a Winchester

.300 rifle. We used trees and rocks for cover and stumbled down the hillside for about half a mile, then came across belts of machine gun ammunition and the plane's cockpit hatch. A full search of the woods was impossible so we returned to the remains of the crashed plane.

The RAF officer was examining all parts of the wrecked plane, making notes and removing metal tabs, and as he clambered over what appeared to be a huge cinder I told him that he had just walked over the remains of the missing airman.

The dead Germans were interred in the Leek Cemetery and later removed to a Military Cemetery on Cannock Chase and I understand that some of them have now been returned to Germany.

Ernest Bowyer
LEEK, STAFFORDSHIRE

I [was] working on electrical repairs in the many textile mills and engineering factories and foundries in the area [when] I was conscripted into the Home Guard.

Not the usual infantry but a newly formed Anti-aircraft Battery firing rockets. These were new weapons, in addition to the many conventional 3.75 AA guns in the area. These new rocket projectors were to be manned and operated by the Home Guard at night.

The individual rocket projectiles were made of strong sheet metal welded into the shape of a pipe about six feet long and four inches in diameter. In the last foot of length at the pointed business end was a high explosive AA shell, with a fuse in the nose cone, operated by air pressure at any selected height. This was adjusted with a special spanner before the rocket was loaded on to the launcher (projector). There were four small stabilising tail fins (quite sharp to the touch) at the rear end. There were eight rockets, each loaded by hand on to their own two guide rails on the projector. It was like handling a heavy awkward length of household rainwater pipe, and you had to slide it up the guide rails, then pull it back on to the electrical firing contacts. There were eight projectors in a battery.

Thus theoretically when the battery fired, there were 64 rockets hurtling up into the sky and if the enemy planes and the exploding rocket warheads were in the right place at the right time it would give them a lot to worry about. Sometimes there were rockets that failed to leave the firing rails if they had not been loaded on to the contacts correctly.

For the first few times we trained on dummy machines with dummy 'rounds' in the Huddersfield Territorials' drill hall. We practised loading the rockets correctly and aiming the projectors by means of two-man teams operating large hand wheels whilst standing on either side of the roofed-over platform. One man controlled the bearing read off on a dial marked in degrees, indicated by a pointer. The elevation was similarly controlled and set by the number two man on the other side of the platform. Communication was by earphone and microphone to each other and from the Control Centre.

We practised loading and unloading, and training the projector at imaginary targets in the rafters of the hall. I remember the corporal's little joke, about pulling the rockets back on to the firing contacts with finger and thumb on the tail fin, not with the more comfortable and natural overhand grip. Then, he said, in the event of a premature firing we would only lose a finger and thumb and not a whole hand. At least I think he was joking.

After we had loaded the rockets, swivelled about on various bearings and up and down on many different elevations, we were ordered to stand by and then to fire. The number one man then rammed down the firing lever, which electrically connected the rockets to the firing current, and we then started the whole thing again. At the end of the drill practice evenings we went home well pleased.

Then we went operational. Duty at a battery three nights a week. We carried on practising with the dummy rounds but the real ones were stored in a bunker near each projector, which were about 30 yards apart. We never fired in anger, though we stood by with enemy planes overhead several times. The reason was that the area for miles around was residential and to fire over the houses could have caused a lot of damage as the empty metal rocket fuel containers fell from the sky on to the rooftops. The Jerries always seemed unsporting in occupying sky that we were not allowed to fire into.

We did practise live fire once. It was a glorious 'summer' day in November and we were taken by train and lorry to Hornsea on the North Yorkshire coast. Each platoon went in turn to the projectors lined up on the cliff top and loaded live rockets (I was worried about my fingers) and fired a salvo into the sky over the sea. I was never more scared in my life. Great 30-foot-long sheets of flame past our heads and a roar like an express train in a tunnel, and the flimsy metal structure of the platform of the projector shaking and resonating; and us almost too shocked and deaf to hear the commands to check for misfires and turn to a neutral bearing.

Then it was the turn of the next platoon. We staggered to the rear, nursing our eardrums and chattering excitedly as we watched them perform. On the way back we had a good booze up provided by some benefactor who had supplied crates of beer on the train.

After a few more weeks as a routine member of a projector team, I was sent to the Radar Plotting Room. At first I thought this was because I was super intelligent and had electrical experience but my ego was quickly deflated when I was told it was because I lived near the gunsite that controlled the firing of all the AA Batteries in the area.

The job was simple and much more comfortable than being an active 'gunner'. It entailed turning a handle mounted on the side of a large table about six feet square, which moved a pointer over a scale map of the area, under a glass cover on the table. Another man controlled the 'East–West Movement', complementing my 'North–South' handle. Somewhere other bods were calculating the height and speed of the planes and the wind direction and speed. Eventually, after all things considered, the officer in Charge gave the orders for the appropriate guns and rocket projectors to fire.

After the practice drills one man was detailed to stand by in the plotting room in case of an alert. I was on this duty one night and the phone rang. In my incompetent eagerness to answer it, I knocked over a quart jug of cocoa placed on the desk by the cookhouse orderly, and soaked the desk and papers and floor.

I can't remember now after all these years what I used to mop up the mess. In my law-abiding civilian naivety I was afraid of severe disciplinary action being taken against me. I had left the phone off the cradle and when I picked it up later it was dead. I have no idea what message I was supposed to have received and recorded on the impressive military forms, now cocoa flavoured, on the desk. There was no method of calling headquarters that I knew of. It was strictly one-way traffic.

Fortunately the ATS operator at headquarters realised something was wrong as she had not received my acknowledgement finish of the call and she rang me to check. I can't remember what the message was but it was nothing as important as a call out. I was pathetically grovelling, grateful that I was not going to be shot for dereliction of duty. It never occurred to me that as I was supposed to be doing a day's important war work next day they could not even confine me to barracks. We had all been fed tales of glasshouse army punishments, from our dads in the First War, and our mates on leave in this one.

Eric Wall
LETCHWORTH, HERTFORDSHIRE

My outstanding memory of the Home Guard happened to me when I was only 18 years old. My story concerns one of the nights I was on duty at the railway depot at Slade Green where I had been employed from the time I left school at the age of 14.

Myself and my colleague, Mr Sayer, were getting ready for our two-hour patrol of the depot when the air raid siren sounded, yet again. But this time it was in fact our area that was to be the subject of attack by way of hundreds of incendiary bombs.

They dropped all around us. Unfortunately some had fallen into ammunition wagons that were parked in a short siding just inside the depot entrance and close to the road and adjoining houses. My first reaction was to go into the train shed with the object of getting an electric unit from the shed to pull the wagons away from the nearby houses. But when I got to the shed the electric current had been switched off.

I then returned to the sidings where the burning wagons were stood, and with the help of my fellow Home Guards we managed to manhandle away five of the six wagons with the help of a brave action by Mr Sayers who went between the fifth and sixth wagon and uncoupled it so that it could be taken  away. Unbeknown to us at the time it contained naval depth charges.

By the time we had successfully pushed that sixth truck away it was too late to do anything with the remaining five, and they had started to explode, sending anti-aircraft shells flying in all directions. One of those shells killed a volunteer fireman who was only 18 years old, and a school pal of mine.

Unexploded shells were lying about all over the road but we didn't realise this at the time and we had been walking all over them. It was not until 6 a.m. when the owners of the ammunition arrived and were marking off which were live and which ones were safe did we realise what danger we had put ourselves in during that eventful patrol of our Home Guard unit.

This event didn't go unnoticed. We were all invited to a special meeting, and our sergeant was awarded the MBE, and the remainder of us had a photo taken and the story printed in all the daily papers.

Frederick Deadman
ERITH, KENT

While serving in the 4th Essex Home Guard, before being called to the Colours, one of our duties was to guard railway stations throughout the night as the German invasion was regarded as imminent. The railway was regarded as a priority because we would have to rush troops to the east coast if the Germans had tried to land there. However, our Intelligence informed us that the Germans would first of all drop crack paratroops, who would be ordered to destroy vital installations such as railways, waterworks, gas and electricity power. My area was a possible area for such a drop as we are situated ten miles to London and thirty miles towards the east coast. So you could understand the tension that we felt.

We were Home Guard 'part-time' soldiers after working all day at war work in factories and other vital jobs and in many cases carrying out 12-hour working shifts. The idea of going in against crack German paratroopers with all their modern equipment after a 12-hour shift was not particularly appealing. Apart from that, all we had were old rifles and little ammunition.

One particular night I remember that everyone was tense because of the current war situation. I was patrolling the side of our railway station when 'Bingo!' something was on my back. I fell to the ground, and as I did so the rifle went off. I was petrified. My platoon officer came rushing round, expecting to see a paratrooper lying dead or at least wounded on the ground, but all he found was a big tom cat scurrying away. The bloody thing had jumped from the roof on to my back.

I could not believe it, but I can tell you that I was relieved. However, the rest of the boys in the Home Guard never did let me live it down.

John Perry
ROMFORD, ESSEX

An interesting part of Home Guard training was that given by former members of the International Brigade who had served against Franco in the Spanish Civil War of 1936–37. We were taken to a country estate at Rowlands Castle and were shown how to make Molotov Cocktails and how to throw them into the tracks of German tanks. No one seemed to tell us, and I am not sure, even now, what the Germans would have been doing whilst all this was going on. Also we were shown how to put a wire across the road at chest height to throw motorcyclists off their machines plus numerous other 'do-it-yourself' ways of impeding an enemy.

Bob McGill

WEST HADDON, NORTHAMPTONSHIRE

During the war we always flew a Union Jack outside our house. We also had a 'V' painted on our front door. For all of this we were regarded as a little eccentric. However, we were well known for our display in the area by the servicemen who billeted nearby.

Late one night there was a loud banging on the door which was answered by my mother. All five foot of her. To her and our astonishment there stood the entire crew of a Dornier 17, which had been brought down about two miles away. They were all dressed in their flying gear, and more than anything for some reason I remember their boots.

The leader asked in broken English for coffee and directions to the nearest aerodrome, which was Hunsdon. My mother had seven children and felt very sorry for these young men – after all they were

Hunsdon Home Guard

somebody's sons – so she gave them tea because we had no coffee.

Meanwhile my father who was semi-crippled put on his Home Guard uniform on top of his pyjamas and got out his rifle with no ammunition. However, he was determined to do his duty. He fixed his bayonet and after tea formed them up outside and marched them off towards Hunsdon. That was to our nearest Police Station and not the aerodrome.

On the way he called on his Home Guard platoon sergeant to assist. He lived in Rise Cottages, Hunsdon and his name was Len Bayford.

However, next morning our flag had been torn down and ripped to pieces and mud had been daubed over our 'V'.

I don't recall what happened to the crew, but I do still have the cotton Union Jack which replaced the one that was torn down.

Geoff Robertson
BUNTINGFORD, HERTFORDSHIRE

At the height of the Home Guard power we were about a million strong and I always like to think we would have defended our beloved country to the last, amateurs though we were. My greatest memory of those dreadful times concerns the great Churchill.

We in London had taken a terrible thrashing during a couple of months of continuous nightly bombardment. Our army had been defeated, we were bereft of almost everything we had, and to add to our despondency, Churchill was about to make a speech to the nation and we were all convinced that he was about to throw in the towel. It looked as though we had suffered it all for nothing.

We gathered, as we usually did, in the bar of the Red Lion opposite our post to hear the speech. It was packed with Air Raid Wardens, Civil Defence, Home Guard and policemen and one could almost smell defeat in the air. When the great man's voice, slow and ponderous, came over the air it slowly dawned on us that here was no surrender speech, but a rallying call, and when he uttered those magic words 'We will defend our island, whatever the cost may be... we will never surrender', the whole place erupted. Men and girls danced a jig on the pub counter, people were laughing and slapping each other on the back in sheer joy. That man was our idol and we would have died before we let him down. Now we would show them. And we did.

Fred Woolford
ROMFORD, ESSEX

PART VI

The Real Dad's Army

'"What does it mean when I give this signal?" At the same time [the commander] made a circular motion with his hand over the top of his head.

After a momentary silence one of the group called out, "Retreat, sir."

The commander then roared at him. "Retreat? Retreat? You never retreat in the British Army. You retire. Now what does this mean?"

He repeated the movement. The men in unison called out, "Retire, sir."

Although I was only eight years old I suddenly had a feeling that we would after all win the war.'

DENNIS CORBETT, ROWLANDS GILL, TYNE AND WEAR

Marching through Hopwood one bright sunny Sunday morning, a group of kids hearing our drums came dashing up Walton Street shouting, 'Soldiers, soldiers.'

There we were, Heywood's finest, marching in impeccable time, chinstraps firmly under our chins, boots polished to Sergeant Savage's satisfaction, rifles at the slope (we had one each by this time) and every man feeling that should the Wehrmacht be foolish enough to invade we would be equal to the task. Then the Walton Street gang saw us, and realised who we were and with undisguised amusement and not a little scorn, lifted their voices again only to cry, 'It's only the 'ome Guard. Look at 'em, they think they're real soldiers.'

Well, you know it was quite some time before one really got to feel that one was part of a National Force. That if the worst happened and the Germans made their attempt to land their armies on our shores, we the Home Guard would become, however ill-trained, front-line troops. For some time it was, I believe anyway, a bit of a laugh. Not to be taken too seriously. I don't think any of us as a nation thought that Jerry could or would invade, even though our Forces had been thrown off the continent. As a result most memories of life in the Home Guard are chiefly amusing ones, of funny things that happened, of cock ups, of embarrassment, but above all of friendships that sprang up, some only for the duration, but some which still endure.

One can smile at such incidents as that which occurred when a group of 'guardsmen' were being instructed in the firing of a Self Igniting Bomb. Sergeant Savage was the instructor and he was trying to deal with a missile that had not gone off. He fired several shots in the direction of the bomb without even achieving a near miss. A voice from the ranks eventually cried out, 'How about chucking a brick at it Sarge.' That is exactly how the missile was eventually made safe.

John Slawson
HEYWOOD, LANCASHIRE

When the Home Guard was formed [my dad] took his turn at all night guard duties, but the favourite one was out in the country at a pub called The Cold Well Inn. Anyone who didn't drink was banned from that guard. He often used to tell the tale of one of the squad, slightly the worse for drink, challenging a figure in the gloom, getting no response, and grabbing hold of a pair of handlebars and threatening to throw the rider over a wall. It was only when he

Clifford Fawcett with his sisters Marion and Alice
ready for Sunday School

actually grabbed hold of the handlebars and his partner shone a torch that he discovered he had hold of a cow by the horns.

On another occasion a friend and I were playing at his house and we found his father's rifle and bayonet. Being adventurous children we fixed the bayonet on but couldn't get it off. Great panic. So we hid the lot under my pal's mattress and went out to play. The result was that my friend's father couldn't find his rifle or his bayonet and had to turn out on parade that night and was put on report. But I can assure you that neither my pal or I ever touched anyone else's rifle again.

Clifford B. Fawcett
NELSON, LANCASHIRE

I will tell you one or two of the amusing things that had happened. We were a small village and the headquarters to the Home Guard was based in the local vicarage which was a big, rambling old place. It was staffed by a Regular captain and a Regular sergeant, who were there always on day duty but somebody had to be there at night just in case the phone went. So it was decided that it should be worked on a rota system, where two men would have to be on each night. The duty didn't start until ten o'clock at night and they were relieved again at eight o'clock in the morning. Being a Home Guard battalion, they always liked their drop of beer and they used to go down to the pub and then come up to do their duty.

These two characters who had been down this night to the pub and had rather a little too much to drink, came back up into the headquarters and we had just received a new Lewis sub-machine gun, so they decided that they would try and see how it worked. They were messing about with it and it went off and blew a hole in the wall – not a very large one but still a hole! They didn't know what to do and then one of them had the bright idea of removing a great big cupboard we had there and cutting out a square of paper and then sticking it over the hole. This lasted for at least 12 months before anybody found out what had happened.

The vicar at the time, who lived in the vicarage, was living by himself – his wife having left him. His name was Reverend Branch and naturally he was called 'Twiggy' and he was quite a character. He was our Padre and he again always liked a drop of beer and was very often seen being escorted home at night across the Common, the worse for wear. He always wore his Home Guard boots and once a month we used to have a service in the church for the Home Guard and you could hear him walking about with his boots on and then at the end of the service we all stood for a minute or two and then after we had filed out we always made for the pub – and he was always there first.

One of the members of the Home Guard was a farm-worker named Joe. He never missed a parade in the whole time the Home Guard was formed but he was a little bit on the dim side and I always remember one evening we were having a lecture and Joe, who was sitting on the front, went to sleep and was snoring, much to the embarrassment of everybody. On another occasion we were having guard drill and sentry drill to show us how to challenge anybody who came and the Instructor was telling us, 'Now you have your rifle and anybody who approaches you, you shout HALT WHO GOES THERE, FRIEND OR FOE.' When it was Joe's turn, he stepped forward and shouted, 'Halt, friend, who goes there?'

On another occasion the officer in charge decided we ought to have a route march and to make it a day-time one. So it was decided that we were to march to a local village, which was about eight to ten miles away and back again. This was on a Sunday morning. He said that the best thing was that we should learn to cook and look after ourselves and so four members were detailed to take the army vehicle to a small sandhole which was more than half way there, while the platoon marched on to the next village. We were nearly there when we came to a public house so we all stopped there drinking.

Later, we came back again to where they had set up the cooking stove, which was a big cauldron, and inside it were tins of corned beef, some meat and vegetables and this was all boiling away nicely. One of the members got hold of a frog and said wouldn't it be fun to put it in the pot. The next thing was, this frog jumped out of his hand straight into the pot. It was immediately scraped out and only three people knew it had been there and the rest of them ate all of this stew.

Another incident I recall is that of a sergeant who had been in the First World War and he was training us youngsters in crossing open ground. He said 'now if they start shooting at you, you drop down no matter where you are – even into this bunch of nettles', which he immediately fell into, much to the merriment of all us youngsters. Needless to say none of us were prepared to follow him.

One of my duties was despatch rider and most Sundays we used to go out on our motorbikes just for practice. I recall one Sunday morning going out with the Regular sergeant who was in the King's Shropshire Light Infantry and we were going round the various villages and we came across a public house which was open. We stopped there and had a drink or two and the sergeant had a little more than he should have done. We set off home again and he fell off twice. When we got back to the headquarters we thought we might get into trouble, he was in such a state by then, so we just left him on the front lawn.

Gerald Cock
STAFFORD, STAFFORDSHIRE

My dad's name was Rowland Hill and he was a few years too old to be conscripted, and in addition he was in a reserved occupation. He was a coalminer, which was considered essential work, but he, like many others, still had to do some hours 'voluntary' Home Guard duty.

We lived in a row of houses overlooking farmland, and the field directly opposite us had trees dotted around it and for some unknown reason a ditch running across the length of it and down one side. It was quite a big field, and the Home Guard used it regularly for manoeuvres and training. I remember early in the war that they were very ill-equipped because they didn't have any rifles, although they did have them later on.

Word soon went round when they were training, and all the women and children came out to watch although it was all supposed to be highly secret. The young lads used to follow behind them, imitating what they were doing, because I suppose to them it was all a great game.

The Home Guard couldn't take it very seriously themselves because the women, who knew most of them, used to shout things like 'Why need England tremble?' and the field was full of cows anyway.

Mrs M. Vincent
RUGELEY, STAFFORDSHIRE

It was in the afternoon late summer 1940. Three aircraft crossed the coast at a maximum height, their ugly profile and radial-engined snouts identifying them as Junkers. Visibility was perfect and we received Intelligence that parachutes had been observed falling some miles to the west. The territory involved was wild and barren and would have afforded adequate cover for an army. Nevertheless a dozen of us in the Amble detachment were sent armed to the teeth with 1914 Ross rifles and all of five rounds of 0.300 ammunition each to rout the invaders. We searched and searched till darkness fell – all to no avail. Well – not quite.

Within sight of headquarters another aircraft zoomed in from the sea, then zoomed smartly out again. A distinct rustle of fabric intruded on the still night air. One of our mates was a particularly aggressive type and bitterly disappointed at the fruitless search.

I could see his eyes shining in the moonlight as he gave forth a wild cry. 'Here's one bugger who isn't getting away – oot the way, this one's mine!'

With this proclamation the belligerent one charged off into the night in the general direction he judged the chute would fall, bayonet at the point. His judgement was perfect but when the fluttering chute came into view, its suspended burden was not a man but a landmine.

Never had a man changed gear so quickly. It was reckoned that in the time it took the bomb to fall 20 feet and detonate, he had vaulted seven garden fences, a courting couple lying in the grass, and a pigeon loft, where angels would fear to tread.

Tommy Wilkinson
ASHINGTON, NORTHUMBERLAND

I was just turned 21 when the war started and as far as I'm concerned the first year or so of the war was what I call the 'barmy days'. Some of the really stupid things that were done then make me wonder how on earth we survived the first year of the war, never mind won it.

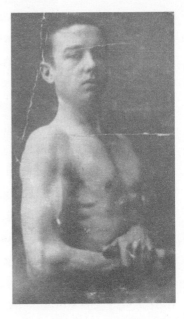

I remember one local Home Guard equipped with wooden guns and home-made spears, and the officer was armed with a sword. I think they thought they were fighting Napoleon. Later they were armed with some old Ross rifles from Canada which would have been okay but for the fact that the ammunition sent to them was for the Enfield .303 rifle and didn't fit. They were also given an old machine gun, which had a label on it saying 'On no account must this gun be used with live ammunition'.

However, the funniest thing that happened with this lot after they got a bit organised was when they rigged this bunker up on some wasteland amongst some bushes. They got some old tailor's dummies, pulled them to pieces then dipped the arms and legs and torsos in red paint to look like blood and draped these objects all over the bunker as though a bomb had fallen on it. It was supposed to get the lads used to the sight of blood.

I pinched one of those legs which had a sock and shoe

on it, tied a heavy piece of concrete to it and buried it in a hole in a nearby corporation tip with just the foot sticking out. Then I sent a little lad to tell the tip man that someone was buried on the tip. It caused a stir, I can tell you, until they found out what it was.

Harry Fortuna
CREWE, CHESHIRE

My girlfriend at the time, who incidentally is my wife now, lived up Brandlesholme Road in Bury, and after a day on the Holcombe ranges the platoon commanding officer, Lieutenant Firth, allowed me to leave the transport at Bury Bridge, leaving me but a short walk to my girl's home. On the way up Brandlesholme Road I saw a boy eating a chocolate covered wholewheat biscuit, which was my favourite. The lad told me where the shop was that had the biscuits, so I called in with my greatcoat slung over my shoulder and asked if I might buy some chocolate biscuits.

'Any lad out o t'forces can have owt I've getten,' said the patriotic shopkeeper, and handed me a bag of more than a pound of my favourite biscuits. As I turned to leave the shop I pulled my greatcoat off my shoulder, and thereby revealed my Home Guard shoulder flashes. The shopkeeper seeing the telltale insignias instantly cried out, 'Bloody hell, you're only th' 'ome guard!'

John Slawson
HEYWOOD, LANCASHIRE

When we were on sentry duty, we were issued with two cartridges and one day one of the officers, who had a tryst with a slovenly, splay-footed, almost lame, ancient barmaid, whose false teeth did not fit, returned to his sleeping quarters in the [Vauxhall Motors] show-rooms. The barmaid worked nearby and every time he was on night-duty they found some corner in which to indulge their sexual urges, or for him to indulge his sexual urges, because it is doubtful if she had any at her age. The officer returned to the showroom via the fire escape at the rear of the building, tired from his exertions and no doubt a little the worse for drink. Anyway, he failed to answer the sentry's 'Who goes there?' and was promptly awakened from his sexually sated daze by the crack of a rifle and a bullet whistling above his head. From then on we were ordered to go on sentry duty with unloaded rifles.

Peter Cane Vigor
LUTON, BEDFORDSHIRE

My memory of the Home Guard is when we dropped on the Fens as part of an Invasion Exercise. Our objective to capture and hold the twin bridges over the Bedford River/Hundredfoot Drain in the area of Mepal. The bridges were guarded by a platoon of Home Guard who put up a vigorous defence. The superior fire power of the Paras was however deemed by the umpires to be conclusive and the Home Guard lost the bridges but it was thought that the defence had been very professional.

In the course of the attack it had at one stage become rather physical and a Home Guard Corporal was tipped into the river. When he emerged the umpires said he was now dead and must withdraw. With a good deal of 'Tommy Atkinese'

he sullenly walked off down the village street.

Later in the day a Parachute Group ambushed a punt full of Home Guard creeping up in the twilight. The occupants were captured and brought before the umpires for a decision on casualties. It was then discovered that one of the prisoners was the corporal. When it was pointed out that he had been killed in the morning, his answer was ready, 'After I'd had my tea I thought I'd come back into the battle for another go.' When the two sides shared a pint or two after the exercise was finished it was clear why the defence had been so good. A number of the platoon were wearing the 'Pip, Squeak and Wilfred' (1914–1918). They had forgotten more about fighting than we young Paras would ever learn.

Major Walter Mayhew
BURY ST EDMUNDS, SUFFOLK.
FORMERLY OF 11TH S.A.S. NO. 2 COMMANDO –
1ST PARACHUTE BN

As wartime schoolboys one of our delights was to torment members of the Kettering Home Guard, especially during their weekend exercises. One particular appeal of this was that many teachers were members of the local Units and it offered us a chance of retribution for their rigours and punishments during classes. It was really all done in good-natured schoolboy style and no one was ever injured or put to any great discomfort by our activities.

On one occasion we were walking along the LMS railway line north of the town when we realised the Home Guard were carrying out an exercise which led them alongside a wooded copse beside the line. Hiding behind some bushes we bombarded the luckless volunteers with lumps of stone that acted as railway ballast. Luckily for them we were a long way out of range and the stones fell harmlessly among the trees. Nevertheless there was a lot of threats and shouting of what would happen when they caught us, which, of course, they never did.

On another occasion we acted as unofficial observers during a Sunday morning exercise held between two different groups of Home Guard. One was acting as enemy and the other supposed to be trying to capture them. A gang of we boys sat on a wooden five-barred gate next to a road bridge that crossed the railway line.

Suddenly a dispatch rider appeared along the road coming to a halt at a place where a white line had been drawn across the road. As he stopped, a short fat little Home Guard man armed with a rifle informed the rider he could not cross the bridge and when asked why was bluntly told that the bridge had been blown up. Hearing this the motorcyclist made as though to turn around stating that he would therefore take another route instead to deliver his message. The little fat man immediately said, 'You can't.'

'Why not?' was the reply.

'Because I've just shot you,' came the answer as the fat man criss-crossed the rider's uniform with a stick of white chalk.

Another time when we were out on a Sunday morning walk, we came across a group of Home Guard men sitting on the ground in a field, being addressed by an officer. They were being instructed on how to foil or thwart any attempts at advance by the German army. At the end of his talk the officer set the men a poser as to how they would prevent the Germans from using the local railway station if it was in danger of being captured. One bright chap answered saying he would enter the booking office and tear up all the tickets. He seriously thought that without valid tickets the German soldiers would be unable to use the trains.

Hidden away all over the rural countryside there were many pill-boxes, strongpoints, underground bunkers and similar places where the Home Guard would set up road blocks or defensive positions in the event of invasion. Obviously the keen eyes of schoolboy wanderers knew where most of these were and we would go searching round them, especially during school holidays when the potential defenders were otherwise engaged. Our search was for weapons, phosphorus bombs and any other devices which rumour had it had been buried in

stockpiles close to the strongpoints. We did an immense amount of digging, all very fruitless, fortunately for us. It certainly lent emphasis to the call to 'Dig for Victory'!

Allah H. Buksh
KETTERING, NORTHANTS

After the V1s we had the V2 rockets dropping around us. So they started us on light rescue work because by now of course the invasion threat had gone. Being the youngest they used to hide me under a pile of rubble in a bombed out cinema, and then another group would have to find me. When they did they had to tie me on a stretcher and get me over the high walls on to the road. As most of them were old men I wasn't too happy about this arrangement.

Frank Taylor
ROMFORD, ESSEX

Washing my enamel mug and plate in a stream running nearby I looked upstream and saw some comrades answering a call of nature. Downstream another colleague, soaked to the skin, as we all were then by the incessant rain, fell in that same stream and sitting up explained 'I'm soaked to the bloody skin'. Actually I think he actually put more water into the stream than his greatcoat and battle dress soaked up.

Later that day as we were nearing Whitefield ready to do battle, Douglas Taylor (later to join the Royal Marines) and myself acting as stretcher bearers came under attack by a group of over-enthusiastic unarmed combat squaddies from the defending forces. Had there been any of our own troops around able to carry the stretcher I personally would have gratefully climbed on it. Instead the day's exercise having been cancelled (again) we trudged our weary way back to Heywood, to be drenched still further by sheets of rainwater thrown up by passing cars taking the officers back to the drill hall. I can tell you that we gave them a salute that doesn't appear in any army manual.

John Slawson
HEYWOOD, LANCASHIRE

Later I remember that a scheme came into operation whereby ex-coalminers serving in the Forces could get a 'class B' release to go back to work in the mines, but only on condition that they joined the local

Home Guard units. One such return member of our unit I remember being issued with a Sten sub-machine gun. He promptly arranged with an army pal coming home on leave to bring ammunition with him which fitted the Sten gun. I should mention at this point that we were required to keep our weapons at our homes. The result of this was that this pair then proceeded to go rabbit hunting with the Sten gun. But the only result was that the poor rabbits were shot to pieces with the Sten gun and so were quite uneatable.

Albert Squires
BLACKPOOL, LANCASHIRE

One night I remember we were lying in our beds and one of our members was out on guard duty. The bombers were over when all of a sudden we heard him fire all his rounds. We dashed out and found him shaking. He had seen something move in the field where the balloon was flying and as all the Women's Royal Air Force people were in the Nissen hut he had been alarmed. Next morning we found that it was a cow he had fired at. What is worse he had missed it.

Leslie Owen Allen
CREWE, CHESHIRE

On one particular evening at the barracks, it was my lot to take part in all-night guard duty. The older men who were also on duty that night had already decided who it was to take the various Watches and yours truly had been selected to take the 'favourite' one of 1 a.m. to 4 a.m.

We had all been instructed on many previous occasions that the Enemy could strike at any time of the day or night, and tonight seemed quite perfect for such a blow to be struck.

Full moon, clear sky and a very calm sea.

I turned in very early before my Watch and at about 12.45 a.m. was called and told to get ready for duty. I can remember thinking, 'I hope I can stay awake and whatever shall we do if they attempt to land in Scarborough.' Oh well, the Nation at large slept on, and I told myself, we can only do our best. So, with a brave heart and much muttering, I made the best of things.

It soon got round to 2 a.m. but somewhere between 3 and 3.30 a.m. I must have dropped off to doze for I can clearly remember coming awake and stumbling over to one of the office windows. This was all blacked-out, of course, but this I soon dealt with. I then proceeded to peer silently from where I stood, feverishly clutching my rifle, noticing at the same time a strange dark shadow which I could not account for. Then, to my horror I heard a funny noise which I could not relate to at all. Cautiously and stealthily I crept out into the Parade Yard and there it was again, that long, irregular flushing noise and more fleeting shadows. This was it. No time to lose or all might be lost. I sounded the Alarm and got all my sleeping comrades to Arms with shouts of 'They're here. They've landed. Come on, be quick'.

It then turned out that the fleeting shadows were made by the moon drifting through patches of small clouds and that the strange noises were just the irregular and infrequent flushings of the lavatory stalls.

You can imagine the private hell of Private Mason.

Eric Mason
SCARBOROUGH, YORKSHIRE

On a very dark and cold winter night our platoon was on duty at the local drill hall. My own duty that night was to mount guard with another man outside the building. This involved patrolling the building's perimeter and also controlling the entrance to the Hall.

The night was Stygian. Absolute blackness, and so, on hearing the arrival of a car, followed by the sound of a door being slammed and the noise of boots on the gravel drive, we, as good guardsmen, were ready with the official procedure.

As senior guard I called out, 'Halt, who goes there?' The visitor replied 'Friend' and then proclaimed himself as captain so and so of the 4th Warwickshire Regiment. 'Advance and be recognised,' was my next phrase.

This the captain did by the light of a torch. I then came to attention as the officer said, 'Call out the guard.' I knew the formula and so, marching to the entrance doors, I called out 'Stand to the Guard' followed two minutes later with 'Fall out the Guard'.

All according to the book so far but that which was not according to the drill was shortly evident because nothing happened. That is apart from the sound of some talking and laughing from behind the blackout screens.

The officer began walking up and down and I could hear the sound of his stick being slapped against his leg. And then, coming to a halt in front of where I stood he once again, though somewhat louder, said, 'Call out the Guard.' My own voice also became more demanding as I went through the whole procedure again. In fact I was tempted to kick the double doors as I shouted, 'Fall out the Guard.'

This time we became aware of the noise of boots and rifles being hastily lined up in response to our sergeant's anxious com-mands. Fortunately the blackout concealed the sight of the emergence of 'The Guard' but I could picture how they must have looked with caps awry, unbuttoned battle-dress and quite unable to see as they clattered from the bright lights within.

The lights of the bar incidentally – as the drill hall was licensed.

My companion on that two-hour stint of guarding the building stood quietly by my side and several yards from the sergeant and his squad. We, of course, were not involved in the fiasco and thought it well worth being outside on that freezing night and to be the only two who were obeying the King's Regulations. We were privileged to hear the words used by the army captain as he forcefully gave his opinion of the occurrence. His words were clipped and very much to the point as he described the complete shambles. After which he then threatened the sergeant with Court Martial. I believe the rules made that a possibility during the war. I do not remember the outcome but when my two-hour duty was over I also made my way to the bar where our Corporal was propped. He was also our grocer at home and I said to him, 'What happened, Bill?'

'Ah,' he said and then a pause, 'we thought you were joking.'

Reg J. Warner
STRATFORD-ON-AVON, WARWICKSHIRE

The giant Austin works at Birmingham boasted a very efficient Home Guard of which I am still proud I was a member. One day we were engaged in a mock battle against the Bromsgrove Home Guard, my platoon being assigned to a roadblock. Suddenly we heard a motorbike coming up towards us, and so we stepped out to challenge the rider. It turned out to be a Bromsgrove despatch rider who was promptly taken prisoner.

Our sergeant then considered the position for a while and then said, 'If this were the real thing I think we'd take the prisoner down to headquarters for interrogation.'

With that he detailed one man to act as escort.

'How far is it?' asked the Bromsgrove 'prisoner'. On being told it was about a mile he said, 'Well why do we have to walk all that way? Let's go on my bike.'

The escort readily agreed to this very sensible suggestion and got on the pillion. Whereupon the despatch rider turned the vehicle round and set off in the direction of Bromsgrove.

'Hey, you're a prisoner,' shouted the escort, 'you're going the wrong way.'

'No I'm not, you're the prisoner,' replied the Bromsgrove man.

Next day in work the escort man had his leg pulled no end, but perhaps he had the last laugh. Apparently he and the despatch rider had spent two hours in a pub in Bromsgrove.

H. McCracken
REDDITCH, WORCESTERSHIRE

Another night I remember an incident with an unexploded bomb which had gone right through Boots the Chemist at Ireland Street. The bomb was full of jellied petrol and it set the whole building ablaze. You can imagine the panic as the building was right in the middle of chemical manufacturing. As I was working at Boots warehouse at the time I and another young chap Jock Metheringham (actually a paratrooper who got killed in Italy) dashed down Ireland Street to see what we could do to help.

I remember that one of the Auxiliary Firemen was manning a hose that was just trickling water as there was not enough mains pressure. At that moment the Fire Service barge came up the canal and someone shouted, 'Enoch, we're connecting you up to the fire float.'

'Right,' he shouted. 'Water on.'

'Right.'

Next thing we knew his snaking hose had straightened out with the water pressure and risen a good 15 feet into the air with him grimly hanging on to the nozzle. Someone shouted out the obvious information, 'Too much pressure.' It was obviously switched off too quickly because Enoch was promptly deposited into the dirty water of the canal. He was unhurt but everybody I remember thought it was a huge joke.

Sometime during the night of that raid I remember I was in St Christopher's church with another scout slightly older than me named Trevor Botham. The church was ablaze and we were trying to see what we could rescue. I remember we took a great armful of cassocks and surplices to the Reverend Ralph and I can still remember his quite 'unvicar-like' response when we handed them to him.

'What the hell do you think I'm going to do with these when I haven't got a church?'

Dennis H. Brooks
BURTON JOYCE, NOTTINGHAM

In the spring of 1940 the 'Duke of Lancasters Own Yeomanry', a Cavalry Regiment, was being transformed into an artillery unit and moved into Pembroke Castle and Llanion Barracks at nearby Pembroke Docks.

I'm not sure of our total strength, but when the air raid sirens sounded we could all crowd into the boiler house under one of the barrack room buildings. We had a mixture of uniforms, some in battle dress, a few in cavalry breeches, some in old style tunics with brass buttons and caps.

A member of the regiment was actually Arthur Lowe, later to become Captain Mainwaring of *Dad's Army* fame. We arrived in the barracks in an assortment

of civilian vehicles, two Morris Minors, a Standard 12 and a Military Humber Snipe. We also had a furniture van with the name W. E. Evans on the side and a flatbacked fruiterer's lorry which had a huge board behind the driver's cab saying 'Persil' in huge letters.

Our armaments were half a dozen rifles without firing pins, one Lewis gun which only two of us were permitted to fire, and a six inch Howitzer which had probably seen service in the Boer War, and bore a brass plaque on the barrel saying 'Property of Birmingham Parks Committee'. This was what we had to defend Pembroke Dock with.

When German parachutists were reported landing in the vicinity we piled into the furniture van armed with sticks to go and round them up. We had no contact with the Air Force but when an enemy plane passed over the town we placed white canvas strips like an arrow pointing the direction taken. This was to help our own planes if one happened to pass.

Our Lewis gun was mounted on a tripod and surrounded by sandbags, being manned 24 hours a day, though we were not allowed to fire during the hours of darkness.

The CO did receive a letter from a nearby Air Force station. The pilot was congratulating us on our aiming but added would we please confine our shooting to enemy planes only, as his plane had several holes in it.

Arthur Lowe, who must have gathered valuable

knowledge at this time for the *Dad's Army* series which followed, was billeted in Treforest probably in the Boys' Club or Roman Catholic Church Hall until 1941. Looking back we must have been the original 'Dad's Army'.

Harry Hartill
PONTYPRIDD, GLAMORGAN

I t was not unknown for a patrol to pop into the Jug and Bottle for a quick one... or two. One such person was with me but I did not drink in those days and waited outside and kept watch. When my companion eventually emerged, we walked off, but after a while I became aware that I was on my own and retracing my steps I came on the imbiber climbing out of a ditch which ran alongside the lane we were patrolling. The blackout was very effective in causing accidents.

Roy Elmer
WINDSOR, BERKSHIRE

[S ome time ago] I wrote a letter to the *Radio Times* which they printed in response to a letter written by a gentleman deploring the programme *Dad's Army*, because it denigrated the time and effort made by these gallant men. I wrote to say that it in no way belittled their bravery but merely highlighted the humorous side, which existed, thank goodness, and saw them through those dark days when many of them were receiving bad news of sons and brothers who were on active service.

In my letter I included a couple of anecdotes if I remember rightly.

One which springs to mind is the one about the little sergeant, Sam Ottey, who always slept with his uniform at the ready beside his bed, braces attached to the trousers in readiness for quick dressing. One night they were called out on an exercise. Sam dressed and ran. Later on in the night, having a call of nature, he could be heard cursing – his flies were at the back.

Another time, during an exercise, our house, which was on the edge of the village, was being used as a checkpoint, and I remember being so excited, watching from bedroom windows as khaki figures crawled from bush to bush. When I saw one of 'ours' approaching I crept outside behind a brick pillar to await his arrival and when he saw me, he said something to the effect 'Thank God it's you, Ruth. What the 'ell's the password? Is it sparrer?' It was in fact Partridge.

Mrs W. Ruth Smith
MILFORD HAVEN, DYFED

There were hilarious moments during some exercises on which bombing raids were carried out. Bags of flour were used to simulate hand grenades, 'Plain' for the friendly troops, 'Self-Raising' for the 'enemy'. I well remember Magdala Street looking like a chaotic bakers' convention after one such battle. I remember too one resident of that street asking if we'd nothing better to do than wasting good flour when there was a war on.

John Slawson
HEYWOOD, LANCASHIRE

Having volunteered for the RAF and passed grade 1, I was then disappointed to learn that I would after all be turned down owing to the fact that I was in a 'reserved occupation' and could not be spared. It was at this point that I decided to join the then Local Defence Volunteers. I served in the Volunteers and the Home Guard throughout the war.

I assume that when people see *Dad's Army* on television they think it is a little far-fetched, but nothing could be further from the truth. For example during the first 12 months of the war we were armed only with pick shafts and anything else likely to damage any person unlucky enough to come within range. However, it was not likely to be effective enough to combat the Germans with their automatic weapons and this was quickly pointed out to our officers especially as we were supposed to patrol wide open moorland around our village.

However, our commanding officer – who was a veteran of the First World War – came up with what he thought was a brilliant idea and here I quote his exact words. 'If the enemy lands paratroops in your area and you find you cannot contain them, the fastest runner must make all speed to the gamekeeper's house and ring for assistance from Ladysmith Barracks at Ashton.'

As the 'fastest runner' would have to cover at least one and a half miles to the gamekeeper's house and the fact that Ladysmith Barracks was a further *five and a half* miles away I didn't rate our chances of survival very highly. I am certain that the four-minute mile would have been broken by more than one person had this happened but it wouldn't have made any difference and fortunately the event didn't arise.

During this period of having neither arms nor ammunition the Lieutenant in charge of our section, himself also a gentleman of former experience, borrowed a .22 rifle and ammunition so that we could practise shooting at a stationary target at a range of 100 yards. He then expected, when the time came and we had rifles and ammunition, that we would be able to show a certain amount of proficiency.

When the day finally arrived we marched proudly to the appointed target area which was situated in the grounds of our aforementioned friend the gamekeeper. He had graciously marked out the target for us at the specified 100 yards and we awaited the results of our efforts with anticipation. But sad to say the results were far from satisfactory. Only the gamekeeper's son, who was in my section, came out with full marks.

Our Lieutenant who was wearing a trilby hat, decided on a little snap shooting by throwing his hat in the air and inviting any one of us to try and hit it in flight. No doubt he thought if we could not hit a stationary target he was fairly safe in that we wouldn't hit a moving one. Unfortunately for him he had not noticed that the gamekeeper's son had sneaked away to borrow his dad's double barrel shotgun. The result was that the next time he threw his hat in the air it was hit by both barrels and it must be left to the imagination what condition it was in when it returned to the ground. Fortunately no one laughed more than the Lieutenant himself who must have had a really good sense of humour.

Now we come to the time when we each received a .303 rifle and five rounds of ammunition thus causing much jubilation and excitement in our ranks. What we did not know at the time was that it was also going to cause quite a few problems, one of which stands out in my mind to this day.

We had a sergeant showing us how to load the rifle and how to unload it and this took the form of inserting the five bullets into the breech. Then to unload it we had to pull back the bolt on the rifle, eject the five cartridges, point the rifle towards the ceiling, pull the trigger and the rifle was ready for loading again after we had picked them up and reinserted them in the clip.

Our headquarters where we were practising this was a small disused factory with a slate roof and as we were blacked out as required by regulations and illuminated only by a single 100 watt bulb, things were sometimes a bit dodgy to say the least. Also, one of our members, his mind evidently not on his work, only counted to four when ejecting the bullets with the inevitable result that when he pointed his rifle skywards and pulled the trigger, bullet Number Five made its exit through the roof. Apart from the debris on the floor that left a hole in the roof and a wrecked 100-watt bulb, I refrain from repeating the sergeant's not very complimentary remarks.

Frank Buckley
OLDHAM, LANCASHIRE

B ill was over 30 and about 5 foot tall. I was 19 and 6' 2" but despite the differences we were compatible. We had served in the Local Defence Volunteers from the beginning and in this early summer of 1940 had received warning of a parachute drop of invaders in the area. We were both put on roadblock duty outside of the factory gates, and told to make sure that no one passed without identification.

Bill had a Boer War rifle and I had a .22, but neither of us had any bullets. On top of that Bill was practically deaf. We put the road-blocks up and walked up and down to keep warm. Suddenly we saw a car coming over the hill in the distance and tearing down the road towards us.

'I'll go and question them,' I shouted. 'And you threaten them if they get funny. Anyway keep your gun pointed.'

The car pulled up quickly.

'Could I see your identification cards please?' I asked through an open window.

'Get those barriers down!' the passenger blustered. 'I'm the officer commanding this area and must get to headquarters immediately.'

'I must see your card,' I said.

'And I said get those barriers down. I haven't time to waste.'

I looked across at Bill in the shadows with his gun at the ready and pointed at the car, and he threatened as I looked. I deliberated on what to say. 'That's my companion over there and he's deaf and if either of you do anything daft you're dead.'

There was such a flurry of movement as their cards

were dragged out and I identified each with my torch. I thanked them and removed the barriers.

'You were a long time weren't you?' said Bill. I explained what had happened.

'My arm weren't half aching,' he said. 'Was they Germans?'

'No, ours,' I replied with a sigh. Obviously I hadn't explained loud enough.

Leonard C. Jeffries
KIDDERMINSTER, WORCESTERSHIRE

There was a weapon called a Blacker Bombard, but I'm not sure exactly what this one used to fire. There was another called a Northover Projector which was just like a long tube on a tripod which was used with some kind of detonator to fire Molotov Cocktails.

One Sunday we were on Scarborough racecourse with these projectors. There were 10 or 12 lined up six feet apart like cannons at the Battle of Waterloo firing rubber bottles at a Churchill tank running up and down. Another weekend we went to Ravenscar a few miles from Scarborough and we slept on bare boards at the Raven Hall Hotel which was cleared out at the time.

On the Sunday we had different kinds of shooting practice. One day we had to take it in turns to walk through the wall garden with a Sten gun with I think 30 rounds in the magazine. The colonel walked a few yards behind and at intervals blew a whistle when cardboard figures would pop up from the tops and around the corners of walls. We then had to give them a short burst.

Everything went fine until he blew his whistle and looking round frantically I couldn't see a figure any-where. Then out of the corner of my eye I saw this big square tin come flying through the air and it landed at the colonel's feet. Not realising in the heat of the moment that you were supposed to fire at the tin while airborne, I peppered hell out of it all around his feet. I thought he was going to have an apoplexy. Needless to say a bit later on when he was going to let a group of us have a shot

with his Luger, he counted us out and said, 'I'm one round short so somebody is going to be disappointed.' He looked at me with a cold eye.

While there I was told by one of the other privates of a time when there were two privates and a sergeant in a dug-out on the beach and the colonel was showing them how to throw a grenade. He pulled the pin out of the grenade ready to throw it but when he drew his arm back his elbow accidentally hit the side of the dug-out and the grenade dropped in the trench. Without thinking he climbed out and ran for his life, but the sergeant grabbed the grenade and threw it the opposite way. After he had thrown it he said he'd had a good mind to throw it after the colonel.

John L. Burt
SCARBOROUGH, NORTH YORKSHIRE

Two of my friends and I were taking part in a war game involving the local army unit. This was the Fife and Forfar Yeomanry. It was an Armoured unit who were stationed in Wellingborough. My father had posted the three of us behind a wall in the park near the centre of the town. We had been supplied with bags of French chalk with orders to hurl them as simulated anti-tank grenades at any armoured vehicle which passed. An official umpire would then decide if we had in fact destroyed the vehicle.

As we waited we saw a small armoured scout car come down the hill, and to our delight the flap on the top of the vehicle was open. As it passed we hurled our bags of French chalk, two of which went straight through the flap and into the interior of the scout car. We were elated. The umpire was bound to give us a 'scout car destroyed'.

Of course the scout car came to an abrupt halt. But then to our amazement the head of an officer appeared through the flap, absolutely smothered in French chalk.

His face was purple with rage and the umpire who was nearby advised us to retire as quickly as we could. Apparently we had bombed the colonel of the Fife and Forfars on his way to a Church Parade at the local public school, where he was to review a parade of the school officer Training Corps.

Consequently he had been dressed in his best Number 1 uniform which was now completely smothered with French chalk. Needless to say he didn't get to the parade. We were warned that there would be an enquiry and we were likely to face extreme punishments. 'Shot at dawn,' we thought with some amusement. However, I am pleased to say I heard nothing more of the incident but it has given me much pleasure in recounting it.

Brian Cooper
HOLCOT, NORTHAMPTON

I was 17 years old in August 1940 and I had already been in contact with the enemy by firing a Lewis gun at a German aircraft from the dock gates which were closed during an air raid. The searchlights were on the plane and managed to hold him in their sights, and I kept on firing because the two sergeants who were near me were shouting out to me to 'Give him hell'. However, when I looked round I saw these two lying on their stomachs. They were supposed to be World War One veterans.

Later I was promoted to lance corporal and one day

the Commandant wanted to inspect the six sentries who guarded the Aberdeen Harbour. Alas we could not find them at their post. I suggested they might be in the big transits shed where the night watchman would be giving them tea. We went to find out. We found six rifles neatly stacked up in military fashion, but no sentries. On asking the night watchman where they were, he said, 'There's a good film on in the Kingsway Cinema, and they've all gone to see it.'

Bill Thomson
SEATON, ABERDEEN

On another occasion a platoon was called out and issued with ammunition and marched off to cover a crossroads. Everyone was in position, everything was quiet, when one member decided to have a practice at loading his rifle. In went the clip, but he pressed the trigger and one round flew into the sky. Pandemonium!

Arthur Fairhurst
BURY, LANCASHIRE

It was during the early days of the war when the Home Guard had just fully developed into a reasonably armed and equipped force from the 'LDV' (Look, Duck and Vanish) that a section was formed and manned by boat owners on the River Trent. This was known as the Trent River Patrol and the one in which I served before going into the army was based in one of the rowing clubs near Trent Bridge, Nottingham. Patrols were made down river, to contact other TRP boats, and also to contact Home Guard units on shore. It was during one of these patrols that a hilarious incident took place, which could have resulted in tragedy.

The sergeant in charge of the patrol had gone ashore to make contact with a unit in the stand of the race-course at Colwick, lower down river. The rest of the crew, with the exception of the sentry on deck, were bedded down in the main saloon, under blankets, enjoying a well-earned rest. It was still quite dark when the sergeant returned, and stepped carefully on deck from the landing stage. His first action should have been to clear the magazine of his rifle but alas he failed to do so. His knowledge of the ways of the river obviously outweighed his expertise on the Lee-Enfield rifle. After tiptoeing across the deck to avoid awakening the sleeping warriors below, he sat on the step leading down to the saloon and as he leaned forward to place the rifle down, there was, horror of horrors, a tremendous bang from the obviously cocked rifle.

The sleeping figures, blankets and all, were halfway through the door in a split second, heading for safety, and the remarks made the air blue. Fortunately there were no casualties but as the boat cast off and prepared to proceed up river, the obvious gradually dawned. Where had the round made its exit?

The bilge boards were hurriedly pulled up to reveal a slowly growing depth of water below. After much exploration in the depths, the hole was located and plugged to await repair at a later date.

There was much leg pulling over the incident for a long time afterwards but to the best of my knowledge the 'powers that be' never became aware of it.

Len W. Murray
WAINFLEET ST MARY, LINCOLNSHIRE

Imagine if you can the scene at the drill hall on drill night and a squad under Sergeant Savage, who was the Senior Drill Sergeant, about to be ordered to 'fix bayonets'. Sergeant Savage barked out the order and the lads in the squad whipped out their bayonets, all except one unfortunate lad that is because he only whipped out half a bayonet. Sergeant Savage's face was a picture. The face of the owner of the shortened bayonet was deep red and the faces of everyone else in the drill hall registered blank amazement. The explanation was that the young son of the embarrassed guardsman had been playing with the bayonet, and had broken off part of the blade by hitting a wall or brick with some force. Too scared to tell his dad the lad had just put the now shortened bayonet back in its scabbard and left his father to find out later.

The Sten gun was never an easy gun to handle. That was my experience anyway. If I was aiming at a cut out figure of an enemy soldier and using rapid fire, I only managed to plough the bullets into the ground a few yards ahead of me. And though the weapon was capable of single shot firing using it this way was for the experts. Bayonet practice was something that always made me shudder. We used to queue up, rifles with bayonets fixed, and every man 'hyped up' to do the most awful damage to the enemy using the bayonet.

The 'enemy' on these occasions were two straw filled sacks, the first lying on the floor and the second just beyond the first but suspended in a wooden frame. NCOs worked themselves, and us, into a frenzy by shouting such things like, 'They don't like it up 'em'; 'Stick it in their unmentionables'.

Screaming as loud as we could each man in turn would launch himself at the first sack lying on the floor, and thrust his bayonet deep into the straw. Sometimes it would also go into the wooden floor beneath, which tended to hold up the proceedings. Then he would sweep on to rip the guts (well, straw) out of the second totally inoffensive sack.

The popular belief, which was held by NCOs chiefly,

was that German soldiers weren't partial to 'cold steel' and would surrender to us in their thousands at the mere sight of a bayonet brandished by members of the Home Guard. That wasn't generally the view shared by the ranks.

'Shove it in the groin, stick it up under his chin, in his armpit.' These and more were the exhortations hurled at us during bayonet drill. My imagination though was painting pictures of German NCOs telling their recruits exactly the same thing, 'Ze 'ome guard don't like ze bayonet up 'em.'

As far as I was concerned these Feldwebels were dead right. Who in their right mind would relish being on the receiving end of 18" of toughened steel with the weight of a hulking great Storm Trooper, or even a member of the Home Guard, behind it.

John Slawson
HEYWOOD, LANCASHIRE

We visited Kingsbury rifle range on numerous occasions in order to get rifle and machine-gun training and despite everything no one was even scratched.

The first time we had to start at 500 yards, fire five rounds, run to 400 then fire five more, run to 300, fire five rounds from the hip, which went in all directions except at the target. If anyone has tried to fire a gun accurately after running 200 yards flat out in army boots, when you are totally unfit, they will know the result. We couldn't have hit a barn door at ten paces.

As ten companies usually visited the firing range at the same time, you had to wait quite some time for your turn to fire, so there were various activities going on. The most popular was cards. A groundsheet spread out made the table.

I was sitting talking to some friends with my back to such a card school. The grass was very tufty and I easily pulled a large tuft out of the soil. Looking round I thought what a good joke it would be if I could throw this large tuft of grass up into the air and land it right in the middle of the money on the ground sheet. Anyway the tuft was heavier than I thought or I was not as strong as I thought I was and did not give the effort necessary to reach the centre of the group as I threw backwards over my head. It actually hit the sergeant major on the back of the neck with quite a thump.

He whirled round demanding to know who had thrown it. I kept my back to him and pretended not to know what he was talking about. Luckily for me my friends did not let on either. He never did find out but never forgot the incident and was asking about it for quite some time afterwards.

Another time we were at the range learning about the Sten gun which had recently been issued. This gun made by Accles and Pollock based in my hometown of Oldbury was a cheap sub-machine gun using 9mm ammunition which was the same size as the Germans used. It was understood that this was chosen so that if at any time the army got to Germany then German ammunition would be used.

Anyway the first Sten guns were notorious for their unreliability. They were constantly jamming. We had training at headquarters on the unjamming methods before we had actual firing practice. At least most of us did.

At this particular visit to the range, I was stationed second one in from the end of the line. The first man had not had any training in the use of this gun. Next to this man was the captain, who was watching the company as it was preparing to fire to see the results. We were given the order to fire a short burst at the targets. The gun of the man next to me and the captain jammed. Not knowing what to do he turned to the captain, still with his finger on the trigger, pointed the gun at him and said, 'Hey, this thing's stopped.'

The captain said 'Oh my God' and gave the barrel of the gun a good hit and knocked it sideways so that it pointed up the range. This jolt freed the bolt, which had apparently jammed back, and the gun spewed bullets up the range.

Needless to say the man in question was removed rather forcefully from the firing line.

A couple of years later I purchased a motorcycle and joined the ranks of the despatch riders and transferred from A Company to headquarters.

During a Sunday exercise amongst the regiment I was posted to a Major Threllfall at the attacking headquarters. When I arrived I asked a sergeant where I could find the major.

He said, 'You will know him when you see him. He will be out of the tent in a minute.'

Suddenly there he was, resplendent in khaki drill shirt and shorts with tight creases, with crossed bandoliers of cartridges holding two holsters filled with two 45 automatics. On his head was an Australian bush hat. He looked more like a Mexican bandit than a British officer.

I reported to him and he said to stand by until required. This turned out to be not at all that day so I was left to watch the exercise. This turned out to be an attack by half the battalion against the other half. Each group was situated on a hill either side of a valley, the sides of which were fairly steep.

The idea of the attacking force was to lay down a smoke screen and then charge through it and surprise the defenders. Unfortunately the people who put down the smoke did not first check which way the wind was blowing and laid it down at the wrong end, so instead of blowing down the valley and providing a screen, it blew away so there was no cover at all.

Nevertheless the charge went ahead without the smoke cover. Rather suicidal as they were in clear view and the defenders had Bren guns along the top of the opposite hill, which covered the whole of the valley, so in theory the attackers were completely wiped out. I was lying down on top of the hill waiting for the fun to start. It was a very warm sunny day in midsummer, the local kids were coming round with pails of water and charging three pence per cup. They were doing a roaring trade right in the middle of the battlefield.

Anyway, the attackers lined up and began the charge. One man in the front rank fell over a tree root that was sticking up out of the ground and went flying. Some wag shouted, 'That's the first one gone.' The charge continued, leaving this man and myself on the hillside. 'I've lost my glasses,' he said, 'will you come and help find them?'

So we were searching round in the grass for a pair of specs while the war continued, with blanks being fired from the machine guns and rifles and large fireworks to represent hand grenades going off all around us. We must have been 'killed' a thousand times over. We eventually found them so he put them on and set out on a one man charge down the hill. The wag continued with 'we're O.K. now, the reinforcements have arrived'.

Eric Gregory
TAMWORTH, STAFFORDSHIRE

I was an 18-year-old when the war broke out and first of all I did fire-watching in the street where the office in which I worked was situated. I was, however, soon recruited into the Home Guard on the recommendation

The sergeant in this photo is the barber referred to in the story. George Sanderson is the small boy with his mother and father.

of a friend of the family who was a barber, just after it was changed to the name Home Guard from the Local Defence Volunteers.

My main job was a messenger, using my own bike, but I was trained in the use of arms, drill, bayonet and machine gun parts. The machine gun we had was a Lewis gun. I also stood night guard duty, as well as doing my own day-time civilian job. We used to stand guard on Retford racecourse, using the changing rooms as a Mess and bunks for off duty personnel.

One night we heard a terrible scream after a bomb had dropped, and later we heard it was an unfortunate swan. I remember another incident. Our officer had given orders to put out trip wires as security. That was wire with tin cans attached to it so that if somebody tripped on it it made a noise. Well you can guess the rest. The tin cans started to rattle. Those of us who hadn't been informed turned out and 'arrested' the officer.

I remember on another occasion mounting the Retort Tower of the gas house for a view of the 'enemy' which was another section. They were using the Electricity Department's lorry, which was supposed to be a tank. But the next thing was that I and another cyclist by some reason I can't remember found ourselves joined up with the 'enemy' for an attack on our own section at the canal bridge in Leverton Road. It was all rather bewildering at the time, but looking back good fun for an 18-year-old.

George A. Sanderson
RETFORD, NOTTINGHAMSHIRE

In those far-off days we invented our very own hot pants. The day before we received our first issue of Sten guns, our anti-tank boys had burned a withered tree, using phosphorus bombs. Remarkable stuff, phosphorus. In water it's quite innocuous; exposed to air it bursts into flames. Our sergeant leant a cardboard target against the withered tree stump, and ordered us to fire the Stens at a range of about 20 yards. Nothing to it – a piece of cake.

Several magazines and many cuss words later the target remained untouched, but the entire worm population must have taken refuge in the calm waters of the river.

Sarge, with a look of incredulous horror, strutted to the target, stirred the grass with a shiny boot and began, 'You call yourselves soldiers, I've…'

Suddenly there was a 'whooosh' and the grass burst into flames. The wind blowing in from the sea must have partially dried the damp grass, while the impact of the bullets and the sarge's toe had done the rest.

To their discredit most of the lads fell about laughing at the sight of the sarge dancing like a demented Dervish, beating madly at the flames threatening to devour his breeches. Happily the flames were soon beat out but the breeks were a write-off, as was Sarge's dignity.

Tommy Wilkinson
ASHINGTON, NORTHUMBERLAND

A shooting competition was arranged against Sutton-on-Sea, our natural rivals, and they were to provide the ammunition. Thinking that each team was going to have two attempts I relaxed, squeezed the trigger on my Ross rifle at the targets on the beach about 200 yards away, and was lucky enough to get most of them in the bull. Captain Wallace from Sutton inspected the targets and congratulated me. Sutton then had their go and most of them missed the target altogether. We having thus built up a commanding lead, Sutton decided that they were short of ammunition and terminated the affair. That then gave rise to the local story that Sutton Home Guard were better at sloping arms than firing them.

Albert John Freeman
MABLETHORPE, LINCOLNSHIRE

Another night during a raid the sirens went and my wife and I and her mother made a quick run down to the air raid shelter in the next garden where our neighbours were all together. About four hours later the all clear sounded and we all got up to come back to the house.

The wife's mother being about 14 stone suddenly says, 'My knickers are killing me.'

The wife being about 7 stone says, 'Do you know, I thought my elastic had broken.' They were below her knees.

Apparently they had both made a grab for their clothes in the dark and each got each other's knickers on. What a laugh.

Dick Daniel
CHADDERDEN, DERBY

One day we were marched to Luton Hoo where, in the park, Vauxhall used to test Churchill tanks. Major Brett had organised a demonstration of a mortar, which, if not invented by Vauxhall engineers, was certainly made on the premises. It consisted of an Enfield rifle fitted with a metal cup at the end of the barrel, just large enough to hold a hand grenade. When the rifle was loaded with a special cartridge and the trigger was pressed, the grenade, the pin already removed, was lobbed towards the target. On this day the mortar was to be fired at the hull of a tank then out of service with the Regular Army. The whole company (after assembling at Vauxhall) marched to the Hoo. I had difficulty in marching because, owing to clothes rationing, much of my clothing needed replacement and the elastic in my pants was slack, causing them to fall down around my knees. This was uncomfortable, especially on hot days like this, and I had to go behind some bushes to make adjustments to my dress and to have a crafty smoke. So I missed what could have been a real drama.

Unfortunately the mortar bomb (a hand grenade) landed short of the target and fell on to a gravel path. One of the pebbles struck Corporal White in the groin, despite the fact that we were all supposed to be under cover. Nevertheless, this incident gave the back-up services an opportunity to practise and show their paces. The First Aid ambulance took the wounded man to hospital. After this occurrence Corporal White was awarded a wound stripe. Maybe he was the only recipient of such a stripe in the whole of the Home Guard. He certainly was in Bedfordshire.

Peter Cane Vigor
LUTON, BEDFORDSHIRE

An outstanding memory which I have recounted many times occurred during the very early days of the war. I had been evacuated from Gateshead to Hawes in Wensleydale, Yorkshire and during those very early days in Hawes I remember standing in a sunlit field watching an exercise by the Local Defence Volunteers, who were later referred to as the Home Guard.

The person in charge was obviously a First World War veteran and local dignitary and could almost be described as a clone of Captain Mainwaring of *Dad's Army*. The group he was in charge of were clearly local men, and they were formed in a semi-circle around him, armed with hay rakes and pitchforks as weapons. This person in charge was the only one of the group to wear any semblance of army apparel and that consisted of a tunic. From where I was stood I could hear the conversation and I remember it went like this.

'What does it mean when I give this signal?' At the same time he made a circular motion with his hand over the top of his head.

After a momentary silence one of the group called out, 'Retreat, Sir.'

The commander then roared at him. 'Retreat? Retreat? You never retreat in the British Army. You retire. Now what does this mean?'

He repeated the movement. The men in unison called out, 'Retire, Sir.'

Although I was only eight years old I suddenly had a feeling that we would after all win the war.

Dennis Corbett
ROWLANDS GILL, TYNE AND WEAR

'Stop!' called out this voice from the darkness. 'Halt, I mean. Halt, who goes there?'

'Us,' said Arthur.

'Us?' There was a pause. The voice sounded offended. 'You can't say that, you gotta say friend or foe.'

'Friend or foe,' obliged Arthur.

A longer pause followed, then I could just make out this shadowy figure approaching, holding what looked like a broom handle with a bayonet tied to it.

'You gotta be one thing or t'other,' it complained, getting nearer. 'I mean, I'm supposed to make you say it.' By then the wavering sharp end of the bayonet had come within inches of our faces. 'You gotta say it.'

'We're LDV,' I answered, before Arthur could complicate matters further.

At the broom handle end of the weapon the shadow became a tin-hatted, white disc of a face wearing glasses. 'How do I know you're not just saying that? For all I know you could be foe.'

'We ain't got bloody parachutes,' Arthur countered with beery aggression. 'We got armbands on, see. Ain't you got no torch?'

The bayonet lowered itself. 'They've not sent no new batteries up. Hold on though, I've got some matches here, I'd better make sure.'

After a fortifying drink or two and ready to take on the whole Nazi army, Arthur and I had set out to report for night guard duty. The searching for our headquarters, a deserted farmhouse amid boggy, misty fields, had us scrambling over many a rutted track and field, to be challenged by this fearless guard now breaking the blackout by scrutinising our armbands in flaring matchlight. We could then see he was a long-faced youth with two prominent teeth.

'Yeah, that's right, you have got armbands on,' he conceded. 'Bit late, ain't you?'

'We'll be a bloody sight later afore you've done,' Arthur told him.

'I've got to do it, ain't I? That's what I'm here for. You never know who's about these days.'

'What was you supposed to do with a bloody spear? Don't we have no guns?'

'Only one and the guard on patrol has that. I'm just watching the gate here, see, so they gave me this. Do you want me to take you to the sergeant?'

'Go on then,' said Arthur, getting back some of his good humour. 'You go in front, you and that bloody pig sticker, we'll feel safer that way. That right, Perce?'

I was about to agree when the youth said: 'Hey don't let the sergeant hear you talk like that. He says we gotta make do with what we've got. Anyway we have real bullets for the gun but we don't put them in, not till we get a red alert.'

We were led through a doorway protected from the feeble light within by a blanket nailed to the top of the frame. The room, the farmhouse kitchen, was full of cigarette smoke and shadow. An oil lamp cast its yellow light over a blanket-covered table littered with tin mugs and tea-stained playing cards. A candle on the high mantle shelf did no more than illuminate a half circle of the beamed and whitewashed ceiling.

I counted half a dozen assorted civilian-clothed men with armbands, steel helmets and gas masks at the ready, standing near to the dull-glowing coke in the huge fireplace.

Looking up from the table was an elderly Corporal next to an elderly sergeant, both in denim uniforms, and both displaying elderly campaign ribbons. They watched our entrance with some interest.

'They was outside,' explained the youth, swinging round and pointing us out with his spear.

As we were forced back, Arthur exclaimed, 'Hey up. I'll show you where to put that bloody thing in a minute!'

'That's enough of that,' the sergeant said firmly.

Arthur was aggrieved. 'Well he ain't safe to be let out. Nearly got us outside he did.'

The sergeant addressed our escort. 'All right, Goss, you've got another hour yet, back to your post. Now then,' he turned back to us, 'let's see, your names,' and he held a sheet of paper closer to the lamp. 'Yes, here we are, the last two. Made a good start haven't you, you two, half an hour late?'

'It was him, wouldn't let us in,' answered Arthur in the same injured tones.

'Well, you're in now, so let's get down to it. Now, my name is Sergeant Watts and this here is Corporal Childs. We've drawn the patrol roster and the night's orders have been read out but I'll go through it again, just for the benefit of you two.'

Which was, I thought, under the circumstances of our arrival, rather decent of him.

Those not guarding the gate with the pike (as the sergeant called it) would be on a two-hour patrol with the rifle, unloaded but with fixed bayonet. The patrol would be on the lookout for parachutists and fifth columnists. In fact, anybody abroad at all must be regarded as spies and brought back to the guardroom for questioning, but what wasn't made clear to me was why these squelchy fields would attract spies in the first place...

Arthur and me had been placed on the patrol roster, my stint being from 2 until 4 a.m., with Arthur relieving me. Those of us waiting our turn for guard or patrol were sent to an upstairs room in candlelight to get what sleep we could on straw palliasses.

Listening to the increasing snores and grunts around me, I lay cold with no hope of sleep. I supposed I must have dozed, coming to with a start and convinced I had overslept. In no time at all I was feeling my way down the dark stairway. The sergeant greeted my return to the guardroom with wonder, then silently handed me a steaming mug of cocoa he had made for himself. As I thanked him I noted the noisy alarm clock on the table was claiming the hour to be 1.30 a.m.

At 1.50 a.m. the sergeant broke off his reminiscences of the last war and, grinning apologetically, said, 'Time to get ready, lad.' Raising himself, he reached for one of the army greatcoats our platoon shared. 'Better get inside this,' he added.

It was heavy and too long for me but I was grateful for the warmth it brought to my shivering frame. The returning patrol guard passed on to me his steel helmet and handed over the long Ross rifle, unwieldy and unbalanced with its fixed bayonet. Desperately anxious not to get my legs entangled in its webbing strap, I pushed aside the blanket, opened the door, and took my first step into waning moonlight and active involvement in the war.

I had never realised, until I paced the perimeter of the first field, how many living things were abroad in those mysterious hours. Startled movements and swishings in hedges as I approached had me tingling with the expectation of disturbing fifth columnists awaiting with shaded light to guide invading parachutists. I had the rifle unslung, occasionally rattling its bolt, and every now and then thrusting its bayonet into eerie wraiths of mist.

The haunting clank of a distant train brought to mind more childhood memories of night – fear...

H. P. Richardson
DERBY

I was a miner and exempt from call-up so firstly I did Air Raid Warden duty and then I was called to the Home Guards. We did our rifle firing practice in the Black Mountains of Brecon. I wasn't very hot at this, but I couldn't understand why on my target they never indicated any score at all. I asked the sergeant and I remember he said, 'You haven't bloody hit anything yet.' They must have thought I wasn't worth bothering with for I was told to go on lookout up the side of the mountain.

Well I was quite happy keeping a lookout. I had a mate who it seemed wasn't any better than I was, because a bit later I also saw him leave the firing range and take up a position as lookout. Then something strange happened. Two ladies in long dresses came up to my mate and lay down either side of him. I thought, 'You lucky bugger. Not one but two.' And they were very close to him, lying there for about an hour but then they got up and went.

When we were called back in with the other members of the Home Guard, I went up to my mate and said, 'You lucky old so and so.'

He looked hurt and said, 'What do you mean?'

I replied, 'Those two women that were lying there with you.'

'You clown,' he said, 'they weren't women, they were monks from the Abbey lower down the mountain. I should be so lucky.'

I think the crowning glory of my Home Guard days was when I was told by a commanding officer that I could be shot for desertion. Our platoon along with other sector platoons were changed to a mobile platoon. This meant that we always had to be ready to move out to an unknown destination. Our wives were to receive special papers to allow them to get their food, for it wouldn't be known where we were going. We lived a mile up the hill from our depot. I was the local 'caller out'. This meant that a despatch rider would come to our house and knock me up and then I would have to go on my push bike and call up the other men telling them to report to the depot.

It happened on a Sunday morning of all times and I had had a few on the Saturday night before and when I woke I thought it was my head knocking. But my wife said, 'There's someone knocking at the door.' It sounded more like hammering to me. I scrambled into my trousers and went down to the front door and opened it. I stared at the despatch rider blankly.

'Are you bloody deaf?' he asked. 'This is it. Get on your bike and call the others up. Tell them to report to the depot. We're moving out.' And off he went.

I called to my wife, rushed on my uniform, jumped on my old bike and off I went knocking the boys up. And you can guess what I was called by them. Anyway at last it was done and off I went back home to get ready and depart.

On getting back I found my wife already up. 'You're not going before you've had some breakfast,' she said, and so she put some morning fry on the table. Well that's what I did. Then collecting my kit and rifle off I went down to the depot. When I arrived I thought it all looked quiet but then a man from the garage opposite looked at me and said, 'They've gone ten minutes ago.'

Now down at Griffiths Town they also had a mobile platoon, so I belted down to the canal to their headquarters but alas they'd also departed. There wasn't anything more I could do but go back home. This I did much to the surprise of my wife and mother and father but I think they thought I should have been fighting by then.

Anyway later I went to our local and had a few beers, and felt a lot better but I didn't know what was to come. I reported for duty on Tuesday night feeling a bit apprehensive thinking of the ticking off I would get.

As soon as I stepped into our report room the sergeant jumped up. 'Right, Private James, Lieutenant Roberts wants you at the double.'

Lieutenant Roberts was a stern but fair man. He listened to my explanation then said, 'I'm afraid it's out of my hands. You have to report to the Lucano Billiard Hall at Pontypool.' The billiard hall had been taken over by the Home Guard to use as their headquarters. Where all the tables used to be was now an imitation jungle where we were trained to live off the land. What a laugh.

I reported there feeling decidedly nervous by now. As soon as I gave my name the sergeant on duty jumped up and said, 'At the double, quick march,' and escorted me to the door of another room.

He knocked and I was told to enter, 'Quick march, quick march,' he snapped and I went in and was ordered to attention and lo and behold behind the desk was a Lieutenant Colonel so and so, the top man of all.

He looked at me with contempt. 'Private James,' he said, 'what you did last Sunday could be deemed as desertion, and do you know the penalty for desertion?'

I nodded, unable to answer. Bloody hell, I'd only missed the bus.

'Yes,' he said, 'you could be shot for desertion.'

This off a man who, like a lot more of his kind, thought it was one big game, who thrived on the pretence situation, who didn't have to cut coal and shift rock six days a week, do half or whole nights' guard and then go straight to work at the mine. I could have laughed in his face.

Well he gave me a right old telling off. 'Perhaps he's right,' I thought and stood at attention until at last he called the sergeant and told him to escort me off the premises.

They had 1/6d pay for a half-night guard, 3 shillings for a whole night guard. Then off to work to cut coal and shift rock. I don't know why I put up with it.

Joe James
CWMBRAN, GWENT

Prior to joining the army I served in the Home Guard for a brief spell. Whilst on sentry duty in the small hours one frosty night, outside the company headquarters (which was an old barn), I remember giving a telegraph pole a few thrusts each time I passed by with my bayonet. To my surprise the guard turned out to find out where the bombs were dropping and why hadn't the siren sounded. Apparently I had done something to the electricity on the telegraph pole, and if I had told them they would not have been amused so it had to remain a mystery.

On another occasion one Sunday morning we were out practising 'street fighting'. This meant running up and down 'entries', etc. I remember one time we were then confronted by a mongrel dog which was snarling its head off, and a few seconds later the lady owner appeared. She looked at us and then looked at the dog and shouted to it, 'Come in, or you'll be as daft as them.'

Leslie Woodward
STOURBRIDGE, WEST MIDLANDS

Then there was the Sunday we enjoyed a full-day shooting at the Rifle Butts at Whitley Bay.

We got off to a grand start when a closely entwined couple wandered across our line of fire completely ignoring red flags and flying bullets. They were either in a world of their own or cocking a snoot at our shooting. Perhaps they did have a point. A stentorian holler from RSM Stevenson restored the blissful couple from celestial regions to the reality of terra firma, but as I said they had a point. If some of our marksmen couldn't hit a huge coloured target, I reckon they were in little danger. Our left flank man had failed to produce a 'chalk' on the target so the RSM took him to the minimum range of 100 yards, erected a brand-new target, and gave him two clips of ammunition.

There followed ten slowly deliberate shots. The target remained blank, totally unsullied. There was silence as the seconds ticked by. Before us a submarine of the Ursula class slipped out to sea. Seagulls ventured back, resuming their endless search for titbits.

Then there issued forth the reputedly loudest voice in Christendom, a bellow of truly frightening intensity. The gulls fled in terror and the submarine submerged at once.

'Tell that man on number 12 target to fix bayonets and CHARGE. It's his only bloody chance.'

Tommy Wilkinson
ASHINGTON, NORTHUMBERLAND

On the Saturday evening it was usual for those who wanted to go down to the nearby village and have a drink at the village pub. It was properly organised and the men who went had to march there and back to show how smart we were.

Those of us who chose to remain behind decided to douse all camp lights when it was time for them to return, so, as it was pitch black when they went by they could not see the camp and went merrily marching past. We were led to believe that they had gone on for another two miles before someone realised that they had gone too far and decided to turn back.

As they returned we all stood there with heavy flash-lights to give them a rousing welcome. The first row consisted of two large men with a small one in between. He had had a little too much to drink and could not walk too straight so was supported by a large man either side under his arms. As they were at least six inches taller than him, they were actually carrying him and his feet were two to three inches above the ground.

So, what a sight. They were marching along to the camp, the short man marching with them but his feet were not touching the ground, it was really quite a scream.

Eric Gregory
TAMWORTH, STAFFORDSHIRE

I was about 11 or 12 years of age in 1940, and in those days children were to be seen and not heard. I used to love to sit in a corner of our room in our little house in the village of Denton and listen to my mother and father and the visitors almost every night. They would talk of the war, the blitz, and my father and his mates would talk about the Home Guard. My father was Jack Marriott and known to everyone as such. His proper names were John Thomas Wood Marriott.

I can remember that his biggest regret was not being

able to join the army. He tried so hard, but they wouldn't let him go because of his job. So he joined the Home Guard and it became the love of his life. He became a lance corporal and something of a local expert on bombs. In fact our house seemed to be full of them, and I can always remember my mother saying, 'I wish you'd taken them somewhere else, you'll blow us all up.' They were in fact harmless and he simply used them to demonstrate with.

You might like to note at this stage that my father was also the village poacher, and supplied I think almost the whole of the village with pheasants throughout the war, with the sole exception of the village policeman. He used to get five Wills Woodbine cigarettes for a brace of pheasant at the village shop every week.

One of my first recollections of the Home Guard was of my father coming home from a weekend camp and telling my mother off until she cried. What happened was this. Apparently they had camped that weekend in a large bell tent that held around 12 people.

When it came to bed down at night, he used to get undressed ready for bed, and like most working men of that day he slept in just his shirt. Being the lance corporal he used to then go around to each tent to make sure that everyone was there.

One particular night he just could not understand why every tent full of men started to laugh and shout at each other every time he turned to leave. Eventually he managed to find out that my mother had taken a neat piece of shirt out of the shirt lap to patch up something else with, and so he was walking round with a hole in his shirt in a most inappropriate place. He was a long time living that one down. In later years he used to laugh about it, but at the time I remember he was very angry.

J. N. Marriott
GRANTHAM, LINCOLNSHIRE

My story relates to Douglas Harbour, when I was a private. One of the worst jobs we had was the patrolling of that area. We had to be on the lookout for any escapees. The idea was that these might try to take a rowing boat or stow away on an empty cargo boat. These used to await the incoming tide in order to sail.

The sentry had to do this duty alone in the blackout, walking along the north quay, the south quay, to the end of the breakwater and return. This was a distance of about two miles.

I had almost finished my patrol and reached the place where the cargo boat was berthed. The quayside was littered with empty crates of various sizes. The visibility was fairly good in the moonlight, and suddenly I just caught a glimpse of a figure dodging behind a pile of boxes. I quite forgot the regulation challenge and shouted out, 'Come on out of there, I've got you covered!'

I don't know which of us was the more nervous. He came out and put his hands in the air and shouted, 'Don't shoot. I am RAF.'

I remember thinking 'that's a likely story' and shouted back, 'Turn around and march or you've had it.' As we marched along I directed him over a small viaduct between two piers to a disused left luggage office that we were using as a Guard House.

'Kick on the door,' I shouted.

The door opened and I marched him in, much to the surprise of the rest of the guard.

Sure enough, he was in RAF uniform. We phoned the police station, which was much nearer than the Home Guard headquarters. The police took him away in handcuffs. In fact, we heard later that he was quite genuine. He had missed the last bus to Jurby Airfield, and was only looking for somewhere to spend the night. It took a long time for me to live this down.

'Have you caught any more RAF lately?' I was usually asked, much to my embarrassment.

W. Lockington Marshall
BALDRINE, ISLE OF MAN

March 1940: A time to remember, or a time to forget. Depends on how you look at things. Johnny and I, not being accepted in the Armed Forces, were quite determined to do our utmost in the Home Guard or LDV.

The Coach and Horses, Bradfield Green

We were eventually assigned to a roadblock on one of the roads into town and, by a huge stroke of luck, within 50 yards of a pub, and by an even greater stroke of luck, a pub which we were in the habit of using. We knew old Albert, the landlord, and his good wife, his son, who kept the garage across the road, and almost all of the local farmers. We were given the evening turn of duty which was even better, so that by the time we had downed a couple of pints of Albert's best bitter, we were more than ready to deal with any enemy who might drop out of the skies.

This particular night we had 'tanked up' at the pub, which had then closed, leaving us to retire to our hut until we were relieved at about 2 a.m., when we heard footsteps approaching the roadblock.

'Hey Johnny,' I whispered, 'who the hell do you think that is?'

'I don't know, shove one up the spout,' he said.

'Don't talk daft, we don't have any ammo,' I replied.

We had, in fact, been issued with rifles but no ammo. It was just us, the beer and two unloaded Lee-Enfields.

'Halt, who goes there?' I shouted.

I should add at this point that everywhere was as black as the inside of a coal sack, no lights anywhere. Blackout complete with only a faint moon putting a dim glow on the area.

'Captain somebody or other,' he shouted back.

'Hey Johnny, d'you hear that, he says he's a bloody captain.'

I shouted to the voice that I had never heard of him and he was to put his gun on the road and lie down or I would shoot. He did and I didn't.

He was indeed who he said he was and we were both commended for being alert. The truth was we were just intoxicated.

Much later on that night we were surprised to hear a vehicle approaching, a big wagon no less, its small dimmed headlights only illuminating about four yards in front of it. Johnny stepped into the road, flashed his torch at the vehicle and shouted, 'Stop.'

It did, and two men jumped out of the back and said

something in German. I shouted to Johnny, 'Hey, we've captured a lorry load of Jerries, go and knock old Albert up at the pub and use his phone to get someone out here while I keep 'em covered,' which he did.

The driver of the lorry then jumped out and said in English, 'What the bloody hell's going on?' To which I replied that if he made one more move I would shoot him. He didn't know the gun wasn't loaded so he didn't move. After what seemed hours, a car drove up and out stepped the captain, who approached the vehicle with a hand gun and after a short conversation he came back to tell us that we had stopped a lorry load of Polish soldiers on their way to Doddington Hall camp where they were to be stationed, and could he now go to bed and would we carry on with the good work.

Eric H. Wilson
CREWE, CHESHIRE

One day we were probing 'enemy' lines somewhere near Someries Castle when one private cautioned us that the next L-shaped field usually contained a big black bull of uncertain temper. The private lived in a nearby village, so we took his word for it and proceeded cautiously. No bull was visible so Sergeant Metcalfe, to shame us for being cowardly, started out on all fours to cross the field to the land which would, according to the map, lead us to near the enemy's position. The sergeant was about 20 yards in front of us and he turned to signal us to advance when, from the part hidden by the hedge, the bull slowly emerged and then, catching sight of the intruder, charged towards us.

We had a few yards' start on the sergeant and we managed to scramble over the hedge quite easily, but it was nip and tuck for the sergeant, who probably owes his life to the fact that he was a champion sprinter in his youth and had kept himself in trim. Sergeant Metcalfe was a non-swearing, non-drinking, non-commissioned officer. Well, non-swearing except for that occasion, for he let fly. His target was not the bull but his platoon.

'You'd have let the bloody thing toss me,' he shouted.

Peter Cane Vigor
LUTON, BEDFORDSHIRE

An amusing incident occurred one night here when an RAF officer staggered into our little blockhouse during a heavy raid, his face quite pale with fright. He had never been in London during a raid and didn't like it one little bit. We found it hard to suppress a smile when he told us he was a bomber pilot in the RAF and didn't find it a bit funny when we finally had a good laugh. A case of 'the biter bit'.

We had amongst our old soldiers an old soldier called Bill Boulter. He was a man of about 60 and in civilian life was a Bricklayer. One of the old-fashioned sort, he was a dead ringer of Bruce Bairnfather's Old Bill from

The Better 'Ole. At work he would wear a bowler hat and the traditional Brickie's red neckerchief with white spots on it. The trouble was that he was so attached to this outfit that he insisted on wearing it with his uniform and one can well imagine how comical he looked. He never took it off even when he was laying in bed at the post. Our officers tolerated all this from old Bill and as he was a bit too old to be marching backwards and forwards to the bridges, which were just over a mile away, they stationed him in the Police Station across the road as a runner in the event of any emergency happening that we should know about.

One night the Police spotted a parachute mine coming down and instructed Bill to warn us at once but by the time poor old Bill had galloped down the road, run up about 30 stairs to the top floor of our building, he was well and truly done up and passed out on the floor of the company office for about ten minutes.

However, halfway through the ten minutes there was a God Almighty explosion outside and half the road fell down a block away. When Bill came to he shouted his warning and was quite hurt when we told him it had already happened.

We had another Quaint Character called Ted Ford. He was a little old man, barely five feet high, who was given the job of running the canteen. During the raids Ted always served tea and cakes with his steel helmet on. This particular night three of us came in from outside, hungry and thirsty, and found the canteen deserted. We chortled with delight as we poured out what we fondly imagined was free tea and cakes but where was Ted? Despite the air raid racket going on outside we were having a good old laugh at Ted's expense. 'Poor little sod,' we said to each other, 'must have shot off home in fright.' All of a sudden a little cupboard door behind us opened and a loud voice said, 'Oh no, Ted Ford ain't windy and he ain't hopped it off home either. He's just been bloody watching you lot nicking my tea and cakes.' He had taken cover in this tiny cupboard and was sitting cross-legged inside looking for all the world like a garden gnome with a tin hat on.

Fred Woolford
ROMFORD, ESSEX

One incident I recall, which still gives me a chuckle was the occasion when three German POWs escaped from their camp near Manchester. That evening the platoon gathered at our headquarters, which was the cotton mill canteen, and we were given the descriptions of these men by two important-looking army officers wearing pistols. Nothing like this had occurred in the village for years, so in this tense atmosphere we were given our instructions where to search.

We were soon setting out in groups to begin our search. By this time I was an NCO and was put in charge of four other Home Guard men.

We each carried a rifle, all unloaded, and in my pocket was five rounds of ammunition, which had been given to me. Whether they were meant for the enemy or for ourselves I can't be sure.

We staggered on our way across fields and silent lanes. It was rather eerie as it was a moonless night and with the blackout being in force it was pretty dark and creepy.

After we had left the village behind us we came to an air raid shelter in the corner of a field which was meant to provide shelter for the workers at a nearby woollen mill.

We paused here and I spoke to one of the men. 'Go down and see if anybody is there.'

The reply was in the negative and also unprintable. I asked each man in turn and all flatly refused.

Now this placed me in an awkward position for these men were mostly elderly and obviously resented being given an order by a young teenager. Some had fought in a previous war long before I was born.

I felt after some moments that I must therefore set an example to the men so, approaching the shelter, I peered down the steps leading to the entrance. In a polite, nervous, loud whisper I asked, 'Is there anybody there?'

There was complete silence so seemingly satisfied I led the men away to continue our search thinking to myself how clever I had been getting myself out of such an embarrassing situation.

I have to smile to myself now all these years later. What, I ask myself, would have resulted if my whispered question had been answered with a short, sharp 'Nein'.

Jack Whitford
WEMBLEY, MIDDLESEX

Our heavy armament and only anti-tank weapon, consisted of the Blacker Bombard, a spigot mortar which slung a 16–20 pound bomb at low trajectory with a range of around 800 yards. I would say the man who designed the camel had some part in designing the Bombard. It was ugly, heavy, cumbersome and totally useless.

None of us ever broke into a gallop carrying the weapon to its allotted position, which was in a concealed hedge, commanding a wide field of fire above Stakeford Bridge and the River Wansbeck. That was, of course, assuming the enemy came from the seaward. Should they attack from the west we would have availed ourselves of our secret weapon – Rusty Dodds. Rusty, a ginger-haired

Samson, would probably have beaten the enemy to death with one of the mortar's ponderous tubular legs. His party trick was to heave the body of the mortar on to one massive shoulder and march up the steep Stakeford Bank, as if he were carrying a bag of feathers.

One day I remember, for practice purposes, a team of volunteers offered to tow a mock-up tank across the horizon. Judging by the length of the two lines, they had little faith in the accuracy of our shooting. The first bomb sailed over their heads but the second, on-line with target, fell short, skipped on the grass to deviate directly towards the volunteers, who ran for their lives with the bomb in close pursuit. They managed to dodge the bomb but it wasn't their lucky day. The mock-up tank, deciding that what the bomb could do, it could do better, took up the pursuit till a tree halted its progress. The whole crew resigned forthwith.

Tommy Wilkinson
ASHINGTON, NORTHUMBERLAND

The Home Guard always practised on a Sunday morning and quite often as I walked to church I saw them crawling along the ditches, camouflaged with branches of trees and hedges tucked into the net over their helmets.

On a more serious note, one Saturday night a large bomb fell on the farmhouse near to us and as soon as he had found out where it was, off my husband went to try

WE REMEMBER THE HOME GUARD

to help. Apparently the bomb had entered a cellar at ground level and blown the whole house into the air. There were 17 people in that house all buried in rubble.

In the end they discovered 16 people. Amazingly none of them had been killed and only one had a broken leg. Apparently, however, there had been 17 people in the house and the cellar and the question was then, where was the 17th?

Suddenly they heard faint cries and grandmother was discovered in the middle of a haystack. In the morning all that remained of that house was a copper pot, a watering can and amazingly a one-pound jar of marmalade.

Hilda K. Burnet
HEMEL HEMPSTEAD, HERTFORDSHIRE

One night on guard along York Street I was hailed from out of the inky darkness by a damsel who said she was in distress. In the pouring rain and Stygian gloom, feeling that at last I might be able to do some escort duty, I moved to reassure her. The lady had explained as I crossed over York Street to join her that she was afraid to walk in the dark down Aspinall Street. But as soon as she saw me and twigged that I wasn't a 'real' soldier she exclaimed, 'Oh it's only the 'ome guard,' and then shot off down Aspinall Street. I've often wondered since what sort of night I might have had had I been a real soldier.

John Slawson
HEYWOOD, LANCASHIRE

To keep our morale high, a social committee organised dances and socials, but towards the end of the war a really big event was held in the George Hotel. I cannot remember now whether it was to raise money to start a benevolent Fund or whether it was to celebrate victory over the Japanese.

Top brass from the army as well as from the Home Guard had been invited as guests. I was dancing with a partner I had grabbed in a Paul Jones when suddenly she broke my embrace, went up to a full colonel in the Regular Army, and kicked him vigorously on the arse. 'Take that you bastard,' she exclaimed, 'for sending my John to North Africa.'

I was so embarrassed that I could only stand there open-mouthed until she rejoined me to continue the quickstep. I never found out who her John was or why she objected to his being sent to North Africa in particular. When many years later I thought I recognised the lady, I taxed her with it but she denied all knowledge of the incident, although she had a brother named John.

Peter Cane Vigor
LUTON, BEDFORDSHIRE

There was a very respected gentleman of Knipton, a Mr Salisbury, who was a pig farmer and very well known for miles around for his excellent white pigs. He won many many prizes at shows with them.

On the road from Knipton to Croxton there was a

Home Guard hut and inside it was a bunk. Now I assume mostly two men would be sent up there at night to guard that road, and they would then take it in turns to sleep in this bunk. On this particular night only Bert Salisbury was sent, so his mother packed him up sandwiches, hot drinks and his pyjamas.

Now no one had ever checked up on the guard on this road all the while that it had been used for guard duty purposes. But yes you can imagine what happened. For the first time a Regular Army officer did his round of all the Home Guard units that night.

When he arrived at the Knipton one at around 1 a.m. he found a rifle leaning up outside the hut against the door, and inside he found Bert snuggled down in his pyjamas snoring away peacefully. I don't know what the precise outcome of all this was, but I do know that Bert was very rudely awakened.

J. N. Marriott
GRANTHAM, LINCOLNSHIRE

[At one time] platoons from the surrounding areas assembled for a practice throw. Many of them had never handled a bomb before, and the Regular Army sergeant instructor failed to ensure that the bombs were degreased before aiming. What a shambles. Bombs were dropping all over the place and some failed to go off. One senior officer was seen to march off gripping his swagger stick very tightly with a desperate look on his face as if to say 'if I want to see my farm again now is the time to move'.

One bomb went into the air and was noticed by a little black mongrel which happened to be rabbiting in the sandhills and, of course, it proceeded to gallop down to the beach and investigate. Its nose was about three inches from the bomb and it was giving it a good sniff while the platoons up above held their breath and waited for it to distintegrate. The bomb exploded and the dog, apparently unharmed, gave a loud howl and headed down the beach for Saltfleet at a fast rate of knots.

Albert John Freeman
MABLETHORPE, LINCOLNSHIRE

Training can be amusing as well as having potential dangers. On one occasion we had to learn to pass a message accurately by mouth. A crowd of us were formed in a long line. A message was whispered to the first. He in turn passed it on to the second man and so it went on. For example the message sent down might be: 'Regardless of weather, A Company will advance at 0200 hours.'

When the last man shouted out the message he received it was supposed to be the same as the message at the start. However, it rarely was and the example I've given could easily finish up as: 'It gives us pleasure to invite you to a dance at 0200 hours.' The result of our long messages could be anyone's guess.

Another example of a mixture of danger and humour was when my brother and I were going on duty one dark night and when we came to Church Street we found it roped off with Police and Air Raid Wardens at the scene. I asked why and they said they suspected an unexploded bomb in the area. So we continued on to the lecture hall. There was a lot of anti-aircraft fire at the time, so one of our officers told me to go to the door and collect any of the residents of Church Street who had nowhere to go, and bring them into the hall. I think he was afraid they might be hit by shrapnel from our own guns. In no time at all I had directed quite a crowd into the hall. I am sure there were a lot of people from other streets besides Church Street, but they all seemed to settle in well.

The amusing part came when our officer called me over and whispered to me, 'Keep an eye open on those rifles and that little man who's looking at them. He's a red hot communist.' That little man happened to live in my street. He was a communist, but I could not imagine him trying to smuggle a Remington rifle out under his jacket or grabbing one and running into the street and trying to start the revolution now.

We also had as members of our Home Guard all the members of the Dunston Brass band. At least I think it was theirs and many a time we marched proudly behind this dedicated body of men in our parades around Dunston and sometimes further afield. They mustn't have been available for one parade we had. It must have been a War Weapons Week or something like that. But some genius had the bright idea of providing music by means of a loudspeaker from a military truck driving in front of the parade.

The parade was composed of Home Guards, Cadets, Scouts, First Aid, etc., and off we went to the rousing tune of a Sousa march. Everyone was in perfect step, arms swinging and heads high, when all of a sudden the music over the loudspeaker seemed to get faster and faster.

The leading members of the parade started tearing along like the Durham Light Infantry in a desperate attempt to keep step with the music. It was all to no avail. It was soon total chaos with everyone out of step and so we had to fall back on the NCOs with their 'Left, right, left, right' routine.

Joseph O'Keefe
DUNSTON, GATESHEAD

Towards the end of the war we were given the honour of Inspection by the Deputy Prime Minister, Clement Attlee, and our local Member of Parliament,

Bob Taylor. The Inspection was held in the grounds of Bedlington Grammar School. We gave a display of marching, counter-marching and arms drill.

Marching on the close-cut grass of the sports field we felt like a ghost army. There is something reassuring about the beat of boot on hard road but we must have done well for not once did the RSM invoke his favourite expression of disapproval.

'When I was a little boy I had some toy soldiers. Then I lost them,' this delivered in a soft voice. Then the famous roar, 'BUT NOW I FOUND 'EM AGAIN!'

The colonel was masterminding affairs from the roof of the cricket pavilion which had been rigged with a wind-up gramophone, a pile of marching 78s and a microphone. Even the RSM was impressed enough to say sotto voce, 'Keep it up, lads – you look like real soldiers.'

Unfortunately the commanding officer, flushed by the rectitude of our display, got his records mixed up, replacing a quick march with a slow one. Oh calamity. It had to be seen to be believed: stumbling soldiers; a purple-faced RSM; the C.O. bumbling excuses into the mike. But the audience seated around the perimeter loved every minute of it. In later years I saw Messrs Eric Sykes, Spike Milligan and Harry Secombe do a similar turn – but theirs was nothing to ours.

Later we retired to the Wallaw Cinema where the Deputy Premier told us how the whole nation was indebted to us for our stout-hearted efforts. Then with a twinkle in his eye, he remarked how much he and Bob the local MP had enjoyed our unusual display on the cricket field.

Tommy Wilkinson
ASHINGTON, NORTHUMBERLAND

PART VII

Opposing Sides: The Home Guard vs the Regular Forces

'The exercise envisaged hordes of fanatical Storm Troopers advancing up the beach. One man from each team would, therefore, at a given signal, and within a certain time limit, run up the side of the sandhills and across the top with a loaded Lee-Enfield rifle with a full magazine arriving at the firing point gasping for breath, when he would then pour a withering fire into the enemy who, not being immediately available, were represented by one tin can on a stick.'

ALBERT JOHN FREEMAN,
MABLETHORPE, LINCOLNSHIRE

Our company of Home Guard was affiliated to the Royal Ulster Rifles, which was one of the crack Northern Ireland regiments. We had many exercises with them. They taught us a lot about soldiering. They usually 'attacked' our camp on the estate on Saturday nights. We had to try to repel them, but they always won because they were better trained and equipped and sometimes they roughed us up in the process. These battles sounded very real in the dark with the thunder flashes and blanks and the shouting that was going on. We wore helmets and they wore 'head comforters' to distinguish each other and the arrangement was that anyone who had been 'killed' had to take off his helmet or 'head comforter' and retire. Army referees or observers were there to see fair play.

One Saturday night we had an exercise and I got 'killed' early on, and was told to take my tin hat off and go to the rear. I did but I got fed up of watching so when I thought no one was watching me I put my helmet back on and sneaked back into the battle. However, I was seen and given a stern reprimand at another parade later on.

We also had Sunday exercises in the hilly countryside around Antrim, and I enjoyed these 'battles'. One Sunday I was leading the platoon at top speed and jumping over hedges and ditches, when I jumped into a pit by mistake and found myself up to my waist in filthy water. What I had thought was grass was in fact green scum on the water. I had to squelch around in wet boots and uniform for the rest of the day, and later going home on the tram I stank to high heaven.

Another Sunday we were involved in a 'battle' with the Royal Ulster Rifles. For a change our company had to attack the RUR headquarters in the countryside. The battle went on for hours and the Home Guard was repelled with great 'losses' each time we attacked. Our platoon sergeant said to the 17-and-a-half-year-old lance corporal, 'Take two men up that lane and try to come in at the back of the RUR headquarters.'

He took me and another chap up the lane and we got to where we could see the Army HQ. Then we discovered we had no ammunition. We had used all our blanks up and the young NCO had forgotten to ask for more. We didn't dare go back.

Then I remembered our rifle drill, so I suggested we fix bayonets and try to attack them that way. We did that. Then our young NCO said he was scared to lead. So I volunteered to lead and we crawled down to the field keeping out of sight behind gorse bushes and rushes and expecting at any time to be seen. The army referees of course could see us but they kept a straight face. When we got as near as possible without being seen, we charged the last 20 yards yelling and shouting like lunatics, and stuck our bayonets into the ground near the officer's feet. That signalled the end of the exercise. We had won the battle and I think everyone was glad it was all over and we could all go home. What upset the three of us was that nobody said to us, 'Well done lads.'

Francis A. Dancey
OLDHAM, LANCASHIRE

We had an exercise one weekend when the Regular Army attacked Birmingham. The basic idea was to test the defences. The Regulars were using Bren carriers each carrying eight men.

I was stationed with a platoon on the approach road to Oldbury, down which we were told the 'enemy' would eventually come. This road was made up with what was called 'Monkey Bricks'. These were lumps of stone about 6" cube. We had a supply of these for ammunition. The idea was to try and hit the side of the Bren Carrier and pretend that they were grenades. One of our platoon was a Blacksmith Striker at the local Brades Steel Works and consequently a very strong man. When the first Bren carrier appeared, he picked up a monkey brick and as if it was a tennis ball flung it at the Bren Carrier. It sailed through the air and just as it reached the vehicle the sergeant in it stood up as if to see what was happening.

Just like a film stunt, you could see what was going to happen. He stood up right into the path of this heavy monkey brick which hit him right on the side of his tin helmet. Had he stayed down the brick would have gone right over the top. As it was he collapsed back down into the vehicle which roared off into the night. We never did learn what happened to him but they got one hell of a shock thinking live ammunition was being used.

Eric Gregory
TAMWORTH, STAFFORDSHIRE

We were having our first big exercise and the Regular Army was the enemy. We had to plot them through the village and 'stop' them if possible. I was sent down to the only phone base to take any messages about the approach of the 'enemy'. It was about 200 yards from our headquarters in the Village Hall. I hadn't been there long when two truckloads of 'Scottish Regulars' arrived. No phone calls. No warnings.

They were here. They took me prisoner and put me in their trucks, and off again they went. I threw the Code Book out and the guard at the headquarters had seen what had happened, and all the platoon took cover.

So we rolled on to the next village and so on until we reached a bridge over the Stour, which was the border between Suffolk and Essex. Here the Scots jumped down

(Left to right) Reg Underwood with Alan, who survived the war in the Middle East, and Dennis who was aircrew and killed over the Mediterranean

from their vehicles to do a bit of fieldwork. The result was that I was able to get away and find my way back. It was about five miles, but I knew the lanes and footpaths and I got back about midnight. Apparently nobody knew and nobody cared where I'd been taken.

Reginald Underwood
IPSWICH, SUFFOLK

One morning we were coming down from the hill at first light and soon we were approaching the huge anti-tank barriers at the western side of Dunston.

At the time these were guarded by Regular Army soldiers. In the dim mist all the sentry could see was a party of men coming towards him with rifles.

'Halt, who goes there?' he shouted. At this some of his mates came and stood near him.

One of our men shouted, 'Home Guard coming off duty.' Thinking this was enough, I kept on walking.

The next minute I was pinned against a fence with a bayonet at my throat.

'When we say halt, we mean halt,' he shouted. Once my dignity had been restored I respected that soldier. I thought to myself, 'There's a man who has learned a lesson from Dunkirk.'

The army didn't always get things their own way. On one exercise a Bren gun carrier came rattling down the main road. Just as they passed I stepped from around a building and lobbed a 'grenade' at them and it dropped neatly inside their vehicle. They turned around and looked, but they weren't smiling. It may have been on the same exercise that I thought I'd have a bit of fun with two of them. I was watching them trying to infiltrate us. I was behind some grass and bushes and in front was a flat surface, then a sharp drop down a high wall to a sunken road. I could see them running over the road, making for the spot where I was. One was going to give the other a lift up the wall. While they were at the base of the wall, hidden from view, I quietly crept from cover and lay on the flat surface. I knew exactly where his face would come into view. And so it was as he raised his head above the wall he found the barrels of the rifle pointed about 2" from the centre of his eyes. I would like to have had a picture of the expression on his face.

Joseph O'Keefe
DUNSTON, GATESHEAD

One evening we were told that a really big exercise was on the books and we were to be prepared to be called out any moment. The following weekend I was 'Sergeant of the Guard' on the Saturday night. That afternoon my sister came over to see us.

When she arrived she apologised for being late, saying that she had been delayed by a very long convoy of black-faced troops going out into the country. 'Tonight's the night,' I thought.

When the other members of the guard arrived, I told them the news and we set to and planned our course of action should the call come through, quoting the code-name of the exercise. We got out the list of men and officers, and worked out the order of notifying those not on the telephone, which, apart from the officers, in fact meant everybody. Then we sat down to wait. Sure enough about 1 a.m. the phone rang and the code word came through. Before making a move I first rang back head-quarters and when the officer answered I queried whether they had notified us of the call-out.

'Of course I did, man,' he replied in an irritated manner. 'Why waste time checking?'

'Because, sir, anyone can ring up quoting the password, which the enemy might well know, and we would have been made to look very foolish.'

'Good point,' admitted the officer. 'Do you know you are the only company who has done so?'

Then we went into action. I phoned the officers and my men went out and called up everybody else. By 2.30 everybody had reported and guards were posted all round the school [company headquarters].

Just before dawn I was told to take two men with me and reconnoitre the ground which sloped down to the county border which was where I lived. I took the men who lived near me and who knew every inch of the countryside. Using the hedges and ditches, we reached the houses near my own house. We made our way across the grounds of a large house facing the road, and came up to a high wall. I sent one of my men to the wall end to see if anything was on the other side. We saw him peer through the bushes at the end and then he came back.

'Quiet!' he whispered. 'The place is lousy with men and officers. Two staff cars and a couple of umpires are sitting on your wall, Sarge.'

'Right,' I said. 'If we're going to be wiped out, we'll do some damage fast.'

We had not been issued with crackers to throw but we had the packets in which we had our sandwiches, and so we filled these with earth. Then by a tree, overlooking the road and adjoining the wall, we hoisted one man up to peer over and pinpoint the group of officers.

Having done this, I sent one man back to headquarters to report the enemy's presence. When he was well away we edged our way in the shelter of the wall to the spot on the other side of which the officers were conferring. I told my man to gently lob two bags of earth over the wall on to the officers, which he did with great effect. The language of the officers as the bags burst on hitting them was only surpassed by that of the drivers of the cars when they were splattered with dirt also. We then made our way to the gates, went into the road, and told the two umpires we claimed to have wiped out the Advance headquarters.

The 'enemy' were furious at being outwitted by 'bloody weekend soldiers', but the umpires pointed out that they had only themselves to blame, as they had not thrown out outposts themselves. However, they let the 'enemy' proceed to keep the exercise going.

But again they were in for a surprise, as my messenger had reached headquarters and a strong defence had been set up further up the road so they were once again wiped out. Our company received a special mention in Battalion Notices for our efficiency, and I was asked to become an officer in view of the efficient manner I had organised the call-out. But I had no wish to become an officer – there were far too many inefficient people there already.

I could do my job better as a sergeant and so I stayed one to the end.

James Frewin
SHERBORNE, DORSET

[T]his] involves the Denton Home Guard. It was an exercise at a place called 'Jimmy Green's Pit'. It was a demonstration of firing a Blacker Bombard. It was a bomb, shaped something like a wooden mallet, and it was supposed to stop tanks. It had a special fitting so that it would clip on to a .303 rifle. You could also grip one end of it to throw it by hand.

All the top brass of the Home Guard in the area and also a lot of Regular Army officers were invited to watch. A big target was draped down one side of this big pit, and the Blacker Bombard was to be fired at this. Of course the bombs were not live. The invited gentry were stood along the top edge of the pit above where the target was placed.

Everything went well at first. Every man had been somewhere near the target with his shot. Then one Leslie Doughty (of 'aircraft guarding' fame) had his go. He missed the target. He also missed the side of the pit. The only thing he hit was the top brass standing on the edge of the pit overlooking the target. I remember it being said at the time that you never saw top brass officers move so fast in their lives as they scattered in all directions. As luck would have it no one was hit and the last that was seen of that particular Blacker Bombard it was sailing along as fast as it could down a field of turnips.

J. N. Marriott
GRANTHAM, LINCOLNSHIRE

I remember a weekend manoeuvre when the Regular Army was 'the enemy' in Hainault Forest. We all marched in battle order on a hot Sunday morning for about four miles. I carried the Browning machine gun. The chap in front carried the tripod. Both were very heavy and of course in addition we had our equipment and a Sten gun. Getting near the Forest we all went into a ditch beside the road. The corporal told us to stay there while he went to battalion headquarters in a nearby farmhouse to find out where the enemy was. The idea was that we would set our gun up and give them hell. We even had a wooden rattle to make a noise like a machine gun.

About 15 minutes later he came back looking most displeased.

'That's the f....g limit,' he said. 'They won't tell any-thing because I'm only a corporal. We're not coming all this way for nothing,' he said. 'We'll find the enemy ourselves.'

So we carried on up the road towards this forest and then we crawled up a hill beside a hedgerow to set our gun up.

Then we saw an umpire, who was an officer with a white armband, running towards us shouting, 'You are all wiped out.' Apparently we had gone the wrong side of the hedgerow, and the enemy had been watching us all the time. So for the rest of the day we all sat out at bat-talion headquarters so that was a total waste of time.

Frank Taylor
ROMFORD, ESSEX

In 1941 the army laid on an exercise when para-troops were dropped just west of the town in the early hours of a winter's morning. We manned trenches and road barriers and we thought we could stop them, but some commandeered a milk van which we allowed up to our tree trunk barrier. This had a cartwheel fixed to the end, thus we could swing it across and check vehicles, but the paras piled out and set about us with gusto, and observers ruled that some would have got through. One or two of us suffered with sprains the next day and I heard of a couple of chaps who had to have the day off work. The professional boys certainly made it realistic, and when I went into the forces, we had a night exercise down at the village in Hampshire with the local Home Guard and we gave them a hard time too.

Roy Elmer
WINDSOR, BERKSHIRE

One wintry cold and snowy weekend we, the Birch Mills platoon, were deployed in an action designed to beat off an attack on the factory launched by the headquarters company at Middleton. Along with Sergeant Ernie Rockett, an ex-army NCO and now NCO again in another war, a small group of us were placed in a forward position. Our task was to spot and identify the 'enemy' forces expected to advance towards the position we were holding. We had orders to inform our headquarters command (in the works canteen), where the 'brass' were comfortably situated and well supplied with rum and coffee, of all enemy movements. We were then supposed to delay their advance until reinforcements could be persuaded to brave the bitter weather and move to meet the attacking forces.

There we were, crouched in a snow-filled ditch, rifles (one between three) at the ready. Our chinstraps were firmly under our chins, our capes were covering our greatcoats, and our boots were also rapidly filling up with melting snow. All of us were feeling frozen, wet and thoroughly browned off. We didn't know when the attack would start, only that it would start some time and woe betide us if we were caught napping and failed to give the alarm. Three hours later, three long miserable hours, Sergeant Rockett, who had even frightened us with his threats of what he planned to do with

the 'enemy' when they showed up, exploded: 'What a bloody way to fight a bloody war. I've had enough. Let's bugger off and have a brew. If they come now they can have the bloody factory and bloody Birch too.'

Shaking the snow from our shoulders and rubbing some circulation back into our frozen limbs we withdrew along the road to the Works Canteen where with the help of pots of brew we thawed out and talked about the day's action or rather the lack of it. I don't recall ever being told why the threatened attack never took place.

John Slawson
HEYWOOD, LANCASHIRE

On the grenade range we had several scares. The target to throw at was 40 yards away and we had to fuse our own Mills bombs. There were two types of fuses. One of them was several seconds shorter than the other. We were in a pit surrounded by sandbags, but many a time a chap slipped and the bomb went only 10 yards away. What a dive then.

One year we had a mock invasion of the town by the army as the 'enemy'. The RAF were supposed to bomb certain town targets such as bridges with flour bombs. There were tanks racing everywhere and we were issued with blank ammunition and thunder flashes and ordered to guard the works until the end.

At first it was very quiet around the works and then suddenly the army broke through the town guard and entered the works, all of this while people were working. But we were ready.

We had fixed up fire hoses and caught them all full blast and then ran like hell to some derelict workshops.

Leslie Owen Allen
CREWE, CHESHIRE

B utlins Camp at Scarborough was at the time occupied by the RAF Regiment and our Home Guard battalion was designated to attack and occupy the camp as part of one of our exercises. Our Lewis gun team was spread out on a patch of grass at a crossroads by the Datterel Hotel about a mile from Butlins. Apparently we were supposed to be on the lookout for spies and if necessary to stop cars.

We had quite a few arguments especially when we

dragged two RAF blokes from a bus who were going on leave from Filey and had nothing to do with Butlins. We finally attacked the camp under a smoke screen and I thought we had done well but we were told that we hadn't been successful. However, the colonel made a speech to us and said we hadn't done too badly and that seemed to be emphasised by the fact that the camp wouldn't let us use their bar facilities. So we had to go back to our own barracks and open up the bar there.

John L. Burt
SCARBOROUGH, NORTH YORKSHIRE

One hot summer's day we were out in full force to repel an attack by units of the Durham Light Infantry. We expected them coming from the west as that was the country side of the village, so we spread out amongst the bushes and grass of an embankment. We kept our eyes peeled, determined not to be caught napping. For a long time we lay in the hot sun, then someone said 'Here they come' and at an extreme distance we saw a long ripple of light. It was the sun reflecting on the brasses of their equipment.

I remember thinking 'I hope you get rid of those brasses before you come up against the Germans again'. What didn't help was the big crowd of children and barking dogs following them, determined not to miss the fun. They didn't stand a chance. They walked right into our ambush. I remember expecting the army lads to be big fellows, but when I saw those Durhams they were mostly small and stocky. But I think that what they lacked in size they made up for in spirit.

Joseph O'Keefe
DUNSTON, GATESHEAD

When I became a despatch rider, petrol stations were manned during these night exercises, and the larger ones were used as Area Command posts. I had to visit some with a message from headquarters and there was always a guard on duty to challenge you. One decided to stand guard with his bayonet fixed. The bayonets we had were about 18 inches long and on the end of a rifle stood out quite a long way.

On approaching one petrol station, I swung into the forecourt which had some bushes at the side entrance. The guard had positioned himself in these so that he could not be seen from the road. Just as I swung into the driveway he stepped out with his bayonet pointing at my throat and

shouted, 'Who goes there?' But, of course, over the noise of the engine I did not hear him and just caught a glimpse of the end of the bayonet in the dim light of the headlamp. Slammed the brakes on and stopped with the bayonet about half an inch from my throat. I will not repeat what I called him. A fraction of a second later in seeing him and there would have been a serious accident – to me.

Eric Gregory
TAMWORTH, STAFFORDSHIRE

My next recollection is also with the Denton Home Guard. It was about a young man we called T— T—, I won't give his full name. If you can understand it he was all right but he wasn't. He had crossed eyes and walked with somewhat round shoulders. He was no fool, but all the same grown ups and children alike tended to make fun of him at times.

One Sunday Denton Home Guard had one of their exercises. They sent about six men up the Woolsthorpe Strait which is a dead straight road leading from Denton to Woolsthorpe. It has lovely trees on both sides for the full length. They were told to hide themselves and to pick off the others in the Home Guard unit as they tried to find them, and so eliminate them.

All were found except T— T—. Eventually everyone gave up and they all went home. Now my father at that time had to go to work by way of the Woolsthorpe Strait, and next morning at around 6 a.m. who should he meet walking down the road towards Denton? Why it was, of course, T— T—.

My father said, 'Where have you been all night?'

'Hiding,' said T— T—.

'Where?' asked my father.

'I'm not telling you,' said T— T—, 'but I'll tell you this. I saw all of you, and I shot the bloody lot of you.'

No one ever found out where T— T— hid that night, so you can see he wasn't so daft after all. However, my father always remembers that when he was talking to T— T— he had his khaki 'side hat' on right on the top of his head, and his rifle over his shoulder the wrong way round.

J. N. Marriott
GRANTHAM, LINCOLNSHIRE

I also remember when the army were holding a Sports Day, and about six Units in the area were invited to compete on the assault course. Inspecting the course on the football field, the Home Guard team were impressed by the most formidable obstacle, which was a smooth wooden wall about ten or more feet high which we would have to surmount wearing tin hat, gas mask and haversack, etc. So we all arranged to meet there each morning at 6.30 a.m. before work, to get some practice in. We evolved a system of stepping into one man's cupped hands, next foot on shoulder, head and over, passing rifles over, then the last man, having the hardest job, would have to jump up, catch the wrists of the men on top, and be hauled over.

The great day arrived and an army sergeant in a broad West Country accent bellowed commands through a microphone as he organised the tug-o-war, etc. A group of soldiers sat near us and one of them kept pulling a biscuit out of his ammunition pouch and munching away. Apparently this was their staple diet, and as his mate was gasping and struggling to get over the wall later on, he shouted out, 'Come on, Jack, biscuits for tea.'

When our turn came we found an additional item at the start; we all had to crawl under a net. This gave us some difficulty, as a buckle on my backpack became snagged. I was stuck fast and the rest of the team were on their way to the wall. I rolled over and got on to my feet with the net still attached, determined to take it with me if necessary, but luckily it snapped and I was able to rejoin the gang and get over the wall without further delay. We then collected rifles, donned gas masks, ran over some raised planks, reached the firing-point and fired a shot. There was some confusion over the result. Some timekeepers claimed victory for the Home Guard, and one member advised of an official complaint, but we were officially placed second and were quite satisfied. One soldier competitor opined that if our last man had succeeded with his first attempt over the wall we should have won. On parade next Sunday morning at the Primary School we were congratulated on beating the cream of the British Army and, 'Of course it's no good seven men at the winning post and one stuck in the net.'

Then there was an exercise whereby Mablethorpe headquarters was to be attacked by the Withern Platoon under Commander Theodore West. A group of men was sighted walking down a dyke side approaching the church, and the defenders were alerted. These men came out of the field, entered the church, and joined in the hymn singing with gusto. After the service they mingled with the outgoing congregation, said goodbye to the vicar, left the church grounds, where they were challenged by the defenders who had drawn up behind a hedge. They thereupon produced various bags of flour, representing Mills bombs, and quite a fracas ensued.

Private Eric Parnish noticed a corn lorry belonging to a well-known corn merchant

Mr Freeman on the left

that was acting for the enemy and jumped on the running board to arrest them. The lorry refused to stop and came down the road with Eric hanging on for grim life and gesticulating to the driver. He received a commendation from Theodore West for devotion to duty.

We returned the favour with a night attack on a Withern farm headquarters. Some of the Mablethorpe Platoon were taken prisoner and marched to the headquarters where they proceeded to light cigarettes and create quite a glow. This brought down the heavy fire from the attackers and Mablethorpe was adjudged to be the victors by the neutral umpire, a Captain Wallace from Sutton-on-Sea.

We marched away, singing through the village, and out of the darkness suddenly came the command, 'Keep quiet.' Out of the darkness, another voice shouted, 'Is that Mablethorpe?'

'Yes.'

'You have done very well.' That was Theodore West again.

I remember the Royal Artillery manned two 6' guns on the sandhills, and they were challenged to an invasion-repellent exercise provided that they produced the ammunition. This took place one fine Sunday morning, the start line being Quebec Road near Camm's car park.

The exercise envisaged hordes of fanatical Storm Troopers advancing up the beach. One man from each team would, therefore, at a given signal, and within a certain time limit, run up the side of the sandhills and across the top with a loaded Lee-Enfield rifle with a full magazine arriving at the firing point gasping for breath, when he would then a withering fire into the enemy who, not being immediately available, were represented by one tin can on a stick. After much energy and ammunition had been expended the respective targets were brought back to the top and the bullet holes eagerly counted. The result – a dead heat. We had about half a dozen each. We all learned a lesson: that one well-aimed shot is worth more than a hundred of badly aimed.

Albert John Freeman
MABLETHORPE, LINCOLNSHIRE

PART VIII

All Comrades Together

'My father really loved those days. He had been invalided out of the Tank Corps just after the First War, and I must say he revelled in reliving the old times. I think he and I were probably closer during our Home Guard service together than at any other time in our lives.'

BRIAN COOPER, HOLCOT, NORTHAMPTON

Class divisions that existed before the war, and were manifest again quickly when the war ended, seemed to melt away somewhat when danger threatened us all. Some of the town's notables thought nothing of bunking down when on night duty with comrades who in civvy street they wouldn't be seen dead with. Mind you there were the odd one or two who used to bring spotlessly white bed linen to spread over the palliasses provided. With air raids becoming almost a nightly occurrence perhaps the local bigwigs realised that they might have to risk being seen dead with the rest of us – literally.

John Slawson
HEYWOOD, LANCASHIRE

At the age of 15 years, but saying that I was 17 years, I joined the Home Guard and at a local school in London Road, Romford we were given basic foot drill before being taken to battalion headquarters at Romford Market Place.

There we were issued with a uniform and equipment, which included an 18-inch bayonet, a 1914 rifle, and

100 rounds of ammunition, much to the horror of my parents. But I felt just like Jack the Lad. We were then posted to a platoon based in a private house in Nashiters Walk, under a Sergeant Tredget who amazingly was no relation. There we began arms training and field craft, and at last I became a full member of the Home Guard, Essex Regiment.

Platoon meetings were twice a week. Parade every Sunday. On dismissal a sharp right turn and into the Pig in Pound. Sunday training was street fighting, much to the amusement of the sundry walkers and the usual ribald remarks followed.

Night guards came up two or three times a month. Gidea Park Golf Course, Infant School in Harringay – at the Bower. There we were amply fed, but food was always welcome, and the odd night in the cells at the local Police Station was not too welcome because there no food was supplied and the purpose of our being there is still something of a mystery.

We had weekend camps at Weald Park, Brentwood and there from time to time it was 'Drop your gun and straight into the Golden Fleece'. Later back into our bell tents before dark.

A certain movement during the night for obvious reasons, and the problem of half of the company trying to find their tents in the dark much to the annoyance of the occupants can well be imagined. The language is unprintable. After an early breakfast, bacon and beans, off to the weapon pits for more training.

R. *Tredget*
ROMFORD, ESSEX

I joined the Home Guard in 1940 not long after I had left school. I was 16 and I served in the Home Guard until I joined the Royal Navy in 1942. My father had been one of the first to volunteer when the call came, hence my desire to join. What I didn't realise was that he would eventually become my platoon officer. We served together in the 7th Battalion of the Northants Home Guard at Wellingborough. My father was a well-known local figure, Lieutenant Jack Cooper.

Our company was composed of a mixture of First World War veterans, men awaiting call-up and youngsters like myself. We youngsters were very keen. Home Guard took precedence over any other social activity, be it girls, dances or anything else. Morale and *esprit de corps* were sky high, and we felt we could deal with any German parachute invasion and feared no one. With hindsight this may well have been a case of ignorance being bliss.

We were intensely proud of our company. We pressed our uniforms to look smart. The old soldiers showed us how to get the toes of our boots like glass, and we practised rifle drill in our spare time. I remember practising rifle drill in my bedroom at home with a bayonet fixed to the rifle. As I carried out the first movement to present arms, I thrust the bayonet right through the ceiling. I can remember that my mother was not at all amused.

My father really loved those days. He had been invalided out of the Tank Corps just after the First War, and I must say he revelled in reliving the old times. I think he and I were probably closer during our Home Guard service together than at any other time in our lives.

Brian Cooper's father, Sergeant (later Lieutenant) Jack Cooper

> Brian Cooper
> HOLCOT, NORTHAMPTON

I remember the lovely summer evenings [when] we used to muster at Eastgarth (in the village) and march to the drill hall. What a rare spectacle we must have presented especially when one or two of the lads got out of step and they would begin 'hitching' all over the place in an endeavour to regain the correct step. It looked as if they were playing 'hitchy dobber' rather than performing a military manoeuvre. Our section, platoon, mob, rabble, army or whatever it could be termed, consisted of 80 to 90 men plus a thin, very thin, sprinkling of Regulars.

We were quartered, or perhaps incarcerated would be a better word, in Nissen tin huts, about 20 to 25 men per hut. Now I know there was a war on and I am sure the rest of the lads knew it too and didn't expect to be cosseted or pampered in any way in regard to sleeping quarters. We didn't expect all 'mod cons' or home comforts but I think we were entitled to expect a modicum of comfort, bearing in mind the fact that many of us had had a hard day of graft before reporting for duty that night and, what is more, many of the shipyard workers and miners and so on amongst us could 'look forward' to a similar day after spending a night of complete discomfort and unrest. But the organisation in regard to 'bedding down' appeared to consist of one tin hut per group of 20 to 25 men and one small 'dead cold' stove (I think there was only one but there could have been two. In any case it would have been just as bad if there had been ten stoves – if, and it is more likely than not, they were all 'fire-less'). Outside each hut was a pile of coke and believe me I am being most generous when terming it a pile. There would be, at most, a couple of small bucketfuls plus an old newspaper with which we were presumably supposed to transform the coke into a roaring furnace.

Now anyone who has ever tried to light a coke fire using paper as a combustible just knows what fun it can be – that is when they finally discover they are left with the blackened dying embers of the old newspaper plus a few still warm singed pieces of coke – but no fire. Even the famed Australian aborigine who, it is claimed, can make fire by rubbing two kangaroos together, would find it very difficult to achieve our objective. Could it be, we wondered, that as well as being part-time gunners we were also on a survival course? In the event we did survive, just. This was due mainly to the ingenuity of the shipyard lads – they became quite adept at 'ship lifting'.

That isn't a mistake in spelling, it simply means that all the spoils were lifted from ships we happened to be working on at the time. Hence the word I've coined.

The spoils I've quoted consisted of bits of coal that just happened to be lying about in the ships' bunkers, tallow or wax candles we happened to be using at work, or anybody else was using. On odd occasions we would strike very lucky and come across a small quantity of paraffin oil and it would be promptly poured into a bottle or a can we kept handy for just that purpose. Anything that would burn would be put to one side 'to be collected later' (for AA duty night), old template laths as used by the platers made good sticks, and so it went on. We were being trained as gunners but I am sure we were becoming more proficient in our training in pilfering. I suppose you could say we were doing it for King and Country and a little for ourselves – I mean after all we were only trying to 'warm the place up a bit'.

It used to be quite a 'scream' on duty nights when, after we had shown our faces at the Hall, we would pop down to our hut. Then off would come our haversacks and our booty (the combustibles) would be disgorged on to the floor beside the dead cold stove. Paper, sticks, beautiful coal, candles, paraffin, if we were very lucky, and soon the stove would be almost red hot. The trouble now was, however, that the fellows nearest the stove were in imminent danger of burning to death whilst those at the back were almost in the first stage of hypo-thermia every time the door was opened. I am afraid we were a bit too enthusiastic with our fire-making for as a rule, by the time we were thinking about turning in, the fire was on its last legs.

The real trouble of course was that nobody in author-ity seemed to give a damn about the conditions in the huts or about the lads 'coming on' in the evening – any evening. Perhaps it is best explained this way. Reveille was at 4.30 a.m. (if my memory serves me right) and breakfast in the Hall at 5 a.m., presumably giving us plenty of time to go home, get cleaned up, don our working clothes and be ready to report for a 7.30 a.m. start at our individual places of work. Our first chore before going up for breakfast was to fold our bedclothes (blankets, etc.) and place them neatly on the pillow. There they remained until the next shift arrived at say 8 p.m. This means that the bedclothes were unfolded after lying about 15 or 16 hours in a freezingly cold tin hut. It is easy to imagine the state of the bed and blankets. They were 'soaking wet'. I have heard of water beds, of course, but I was under the impression that the water was *inside* the beds and not on the outside or on the blankets.

This didn't complete the ghastly ensemble for most of us carried an important requisite in our haversacks 'for use and when in bed'. This was a large piece of clean white cloth, supplied by our wives or parents. This was to place on the pillow (Northfield issue) and leave enough to cover one's face just in case you happened to nod off any time during the night. This was a precautionary measure against an attack of dermatitis. A number of chaps had contracted it and it seemed obvious that lack of hygiene, particularly with the beds and bedding, had a lot to do with it.

I remember one incident very well which in a way is an oblique reference to our sleeping accommodation – or lack of. I was chatting to a chap one evening at the Hall and during the conversation he mentioned that he never stayed for breakfast but went home directly after Reveille. It meant he arrived home before 5 a.m. and that he could get a couple of hours of good sleep before turning out for work at 7.15 a.m. I thought that a good idea and anyway I wasn't too fussy about smoked bacon, which was the usual breakfast fare.

I thought I would give it a go and, after warning my wife what I intended doing, I left Northfield Drill Hall at about 4.30 a.m. after my next duty night and arrived home about 4.45 a.m. I was more than halfway asleep going up our front stairs, off with my clothes, slipped into bed and knew no more until a voice finally got through to me saying that it was now 11.30 a.m. and I had 'slept in'. I had my lunch and went to work for 1 p.m. and a ticking off from the 'gaffer'.

It is a good example of the condition I, at least, was in after my night out with the Home Guard. I must have slept like a log for at least six hours and my wife told me later that she had tried several times to waken me without receiving any response. Needless to say I always had breakfast at the Hall after that experiment.

The thought has just occurred to me that had a stranger entered our hut in the wee small hours of the night he could be forgiven if he thought that he had stumbled on a deep-freeze mortuary, with the killed from a previous day's battle lying in the beds. What a picture we must have presented. We were wearing our boots, uniforms, greatcoats, tin hat – the lot, anything that would provide a little warmth. The large piece of clean white cloth wrapped round many of the heads, keeping the 'sodden' blankets away from the faces, would complete the picture for him only to be dispelled when a 'corpse' would suddenly cough or give a startled jump or something thereby proving that we may have been in dire straits but we weren't dead yet.

In retrospect I have to admit that had it not been for the very poor (bordering on the disgusting) sleeping accommodation I would have said with honesty that I enjoyed my little bit of service in the Home Guard. I still remember the great lads I met. The camaraderie. The comedians or jokers – every bunch of lads has at least one.

Sent in by Mrs Jean S. Davison
SOUTH SHIELDS, TYNE AND WEAR
IT WAS WRITTEN BY HER FATHER WHO DIED IN 1984

I can see it all as if it were yesterday. The place of action was Scarborough, Yorkshire, and the centre of most of it was the barracks, St John's Road.

I was a raw newcomer to the scene, Grade 4, pale, thin, and looking very 'owly', on long, skinny legs. I was 18 years of age and looking like a very overgrown school-boy or, to quote some of my working colleagues, 'If you stood sideways they couldn't see you at all.'

The night I shall never forget was the evening that I went to be measured for and to collect my Home Guard uniform. After much chattering and chuntering, together with other young and eager hopefuls, we all meandered into a massive room of a rather seedy-looking boarding house that had been requisitioned by the Government for this purpose. A very bright and cheerful Second-in-Command, who was in charge, summoned us by surname to take our respective places at what looked very much like a very well-stocked jumble sale of crumpled garments all laid out and displayed on trestle tables.

When it came to my turn, he boldly announced to the full company at large, 'Oh, this one has an officer's waist and an NCO's legs.' I stood there completely dumbfounded, midst all the guffaws that took place. However, I made up my mind there and then if once

I could lay my hands on that crumpled ill-fitting uniform, I would make something of it. And I did.

In the department store where I was employed as a window dresser, we were most fortunate in having still on the staff an excellent gentlemen's tailor. He was an artist with cloth and scissors. His bespoke suits had to be seen to be believed, especially in wartime.

Next day I scurried back to the store and made my way to his department, armed with instructions of what I would like to have done with my 'treasures'. First and foremost, a complete refit of that giant oversized greatcoat; followed next by the Battle Dress top of the Uniform, which was to be made to fit properly, shortening the sleeves (which had a nasty habit of trying to cover the hands) and the waistband to be made smaller. The trousers looked hopeless: these were to be shortened, taken in at the waist and a permanent crease given without delay. The Forage Cap, well, the least said the better – but I must say the army-issue boots and gaiters were quite comfortable and seemed to finish things off quite nicely.

The result of the alterations made to the uniform, although costly, was marvellous; at least I thought so and so did the tailor. When I reflect and look back on all this, there must have been (both at the store and the barracks) many asides of 'Who the hell does he think he is?'

Eric Mason
SCARBOROUGH, YORKSHIRE

In our squad we had a man who was impossible to wake up once he had gone to sleep. He always took one of the first shifts because he knew that once he had gone to sleep the guard could not wake him to take over. We yelled and shook him until he fell off the top bunk on to the floor but in the end we always had to leave him at headquarters until he woke naturally and let himself out. We always said we hoped the Germans would come early otherwise we would be down in numbers by one.

Weekend camps were held at regular intervals to train in operating in woods, etc. One weekend remains in my memory for a few reasons.

A squad were being trained in the correct method of working through a wood. Six men with the leader looking ahead, the following men had to look either right or left alternately, with the man at the rear practically walking backwards to keep watch from that direction.

This was most uncomfortable as you could not keep a

watch on where you were going. This was proved when the rear man of our squad, when walking along a narrow path across a hillside, with a drop of 50 feet on the left down a fairly steep hillside, tripped over a tree stump and flew down the hill, rolling around as he did so, landing in a four foot deep ditch at the bottom that was filled with dirty cold water. He was completely sub-merged and semi-conscious, having been banged about during his fall.

We had to quickly get to him before he drowned, as his heavy backpack was holding him under the water. We got him out in time and returned to camp. He had to strip off and get dry and, as he obviously did not have a change of clothes, had to spend most of the remaining time wrapped in an army blanket whilst his clothes were drying by the campfire.

Eric Gregory
TAMWORTH, STAFFORDSHIRE

[T]his] incident concerns the pride and joy of our company, which was a First World War Lewis light machine gun. We cleaned it and looked after it like a baby. Our instructor was a Corporal Ernie Plumb who had served with the Northants Regiments in the 1930s in India and the Middle East.

Ernie knew the Lewis gun like the back of his hand, but whenever he was doing his best to instruct us we would deliberately act dumb, misinterpreting his instructions, putting the wrong parts in the wrong way, and asking stupid questions. It wasn't long before Ernie cottoned on to this and his favourite remark was always, 'I shall be bloody glad when you lot are called up. And when you are I'm going to be the one coming to the railway station to wave you off.'

Ernie was in his thirties and so you can imagine we were all amazed, and no one more than Ernie, when he was recalled to the regiment. But in view of his oft-repeated remark about waving us off, my two friends and I found out when he was leaving, and we turned up at the local railway station. Ernie's wife must have been amazed to see three chaps waving handker-chiefs and 'sobbing' as Ernie's train pulled out of the station.

As a PS to this story, about a year later I was home on leave myself from the Navy and met Ernie who was also on leave. I took him into the nearest pub for a drink and when we chatted about the incident Ernie laughed and enjoyed the joke as much as anyone. A great bloke.

Brian Cooper
HOLCOT, NORTHAMPTON

I was 20 years old at this time and with some of the other younger lads we used to visit on an evening, still wearing our uniforms, the towns of Ripon and Harrogate. We often got treated to a meal of fish and chips by well-wishers who thought we were in the army. We did not let on we were not. Also the girls we met often thought we were Regulars.

One exciting job I got was to guard a barrage balloon which had blown away and come down at Bishop Thornton – lucky for us near a pub, the Drovers Inn. We agreed with the landlord to use the bar as base and to sleep in it in between guard duty. They were very good

 supplying sandwiches and drinks. I wonder would any landlord allow four men to use his bar to sleep in today. Strange, we took it for granted he would then. We were there two days till the RAF collected the balloon.

Another job was to guard a plane shot down near Markington till the RAF got a low loader to take it away. This time no luck. No pub. We were out in the open, sleeping in the fields, and got army rations to feed on.

Times were hard for getting a meal out but somehow we had a pub meal out once a year. Often there was fun and games when a farm man had a kit check and it was found he had used some rounds from the ten we all carried to shoot rabbits. Also some had worn their boots to work and had worn them out. Things were usually wangled to replace them but now and then some had to be put on a charge and had to take their punishment. Think of it in those days. Twenty-eight men in the village had rifles and ten rounds at home with them. Gosh, I am sure the people would be scared now if men were allowed rifles at home. But except for rabbit shooting I do not recall any misuse of them.

John H. Scoby
REDCAR, CLEVELAND

It was in this hut that my military career nearly came to an end. An order had come out that no rifle must be left cocked, or rifle loaded. One evening one of the men came into the hut, and looking at the stacked rifles of the off-duty men he said, 'One of those rifles is still cocked.' I was sitting talking to one of my mates at the entrance to the hut and when the lad picked up the offending rifle he ignored one of the first rules of musketry and pointed the gun in our direction. He pulled the trigger to uncock the gun and the noise in our confined space was terrific. The blast blew our light out, and I am sure the men even beat the light in getting out of the hut. I reckon the bullet went through the hut about four inches above the heads of my mate and I, but we never found out who left the rifle loaded and the sergeant certainly must have hushed it all up.

Joseph O'Keefe
DUNSTON, GATESHEAD

During an attack by Heywood company and other units on Whitefield, a field kitchen was set up in the pouring rain in a field at Pilsworth. I remember that the sergeant cook, named Rufus Cheetham, aided by Corporal Michael Lydon, served up a meal in atrocious weather conditions that still lives in my memory. In great iron boilers a magnificent stew was created, followed by dessert of apple duff and custard washed down with tea, hot and brewed as only sergeant majors can brew tea. A meal to be remembered after all these years have passed. Sergeant Cheetham and Corporal Lydon were to prepare many more meals as the war dragged on, but I doubt that they served up anything better than the one we ate in the pouring rain round Pilsworth.

John Slawson
HEYWOOD, LANCASHIRE

PART IX

The Horrors of War

'The sad memory of that night always comes flooding back to me on Armistice Day when I hear those familiar words, "At the going down of the sun and in the morning we will remember them."'

FRANK BUCKLEY, OLDHAM, LANCASHIRE

was a sentry at Victoria Bridge behind a police box and I espied my father coming across the bridge. So I shouted to him, 'Halt who goes there?' and confronted him with my rifle and bayonet. His immediate reaction was that the Germans had invaded and he shouted, '*Kamerad.*' He had just finished his work and little did I know that a bomb that had dropped had blasted him from one side of the shed to the other. He was still

Bill Thomson (right)

shaking like a leaf from it, and I really don't think to this day that he took in who was challenging him. He was still in the same condition when I met him later in the day and that was the first time I had a pint with my dad.

Bill Thomson
SEATON, ABERDEEN

We [undertook] our night patrols with enthusiasm even on the coldest nights and although we only watched the big London fires from afar, we had the odd incident, such as the time when a Dornier was brought down on the outskirts of Windsor, and the Home Guard went looking for survivors who were in fact apprehended quite quickly. A Messerschmitt 109 was also forced down and landed in the long straight avenue that led from Windsor Castle, but the wooden stakes placed there as anti-invasion measures took the wings off. It was later put on view in Park Street behind a hoarding, and a charge of sixpence was made to aid the war effort.

The first stick of bombs that fell on Windsor one night, although of small calibre, killed five people and I was at home at the time. But hurriedly donning my denim blouse (I thought it would give me some authority) I ran to the scene. Some people were already there and in the darkness one of them, a woman who was a local schoolteacher, asked me to look at a body lying in the roadway.

I was scared stiff as I examined the still form, and

shouted for stretcher-bearers to nobody in particular. As it happened an ambulance arrived and the dead person was taken away. It was my first experience of the horrors of war and certainly chastened my outlook.

Roy Elmer
WINDSOR, BERKSHIRE

I was attached to the ARP Heavy Rescue Service in 1939. We were at a depot in Perivale that belonged to Ealing Council. Our time of duty was 12 hours a shift. One week on days and the other on night duty. I was a Heavy Rescue Driver, but most of the squad I was in were quite old men compared to me. So in the event of our rescuing people I had to do most of the tunnelling as I was the most active.

Sidney Tibbles (second left) at Perivale ARP Depot

We had a fully qualified carpenter in the Squad, so that when I was tunnelling he would shore up the brick rubble from falling in on me. The story I'm about to write is one I cannot forget. It is and was so heart-breaking, although it was a long time ago.

I was on night duty when we were called out late at night because a bomb had hit a big house in Pitshanger Lane, Ealing, not far from the depot. It was a very cold night with the German bombers overhead, and with searchlights above and the Royal Artillery firing at them.

We got to this house, and I climbed on top of the rubble because the property had been completely destroyed. There I saw a man sitting upright, but I said to the carpenter about the man who was dressed only in a long white nightshirt, 'Here Len, here's one dead.'

'I'm not so bloody dead as you think I am,' the man suddenly said. 'Take these wooden beams off my legs and I'll be all right.'

That we did and the First Aid people took him away.

Now I come to the heart-breaking part of the story. I then went to the bottom of the crater and there with the aid of light from the torches that we had I saw that all there was was a fireplace with a few embers burning, and lo and behold there was a woman sitting on a chair. She only had a nightdress on. It was cold and I rubbed her body for circulation. She was bleeding from a leg wound.

Suddenly she said to me, 'This is my fourth move. I came from Margate in Kent.'

She then told me she had been breastfeeding a baby, which was blown from her and although she was conscious she was quite clearly delirious. However, we were concerned that there may well have been a baby, and so we looked around and suddenly we saw the baby with his head upside down on some rubble. I can still see its little legs kicking away.

I picked the baby up and gave it to its mother and suddenly she started crying, and so did I. It was all so sad. Suddenly she kissed me and said, 'I have three more children somewhere. They were upstairs.'

So myself and Len went to the top of the crater and part of the gable of the roof was laying on the ground. I crawled underneath it and found a gas stove, and also a bed which had apparently collapsed forward as a result of the floor caving in. I called out 'Is anybody there?' three times and then faintly I heard a voice say, 'Yes, and it's very cold.'

It was a very young girl who was very lucky because as the bed had rolled down through the collapsed floor so the bedclothes went with her and she was saved, but unfortunately we were unable to find any trace of the other two children. Whether or not the day shift found any other persons alive I don't know, but I wouldn't imagine so.

Sidney Tibbles
WEST EALING, LONDON

My father, whose name was Frank W. Marshall, was a company sergeant major in the Post Office Home Guard, and used to go down to the Caswell Bay Hotel on weekends for training. My family often used to go down to see him but the bay had barbed wire around it and I remember a mines expert had been spending a week or so checking the mines in the bay area. I can clearly recall at one particular time he had nearly finished his work when a mine exploded and literally blew him apart. All that remained of him was the leather tongue of his boot and his leather wallet.

E. Marshall
MAYALS, SWANSEA

One night one of the RAF trainer planes crashed into the top of the trees on the Denton side of the main Grantham/Leicester road. The trees actually must have saved lives in the village, but the pilot was killed and apparently when his body was found it had no head. The Home Guard were called in to look for this man's head, and we children were kept on a very tight rein for obvious reasons. For three days everyone searched but apparently nothing was found until a report came from the Royal Air Force that it had been found. I think lots of the children were like me. It was on our minds for months. I myself took a long time to forget it.

J. N. Marriott
GRANTHAM, LINCOLNSHIRE

On 19 August 1940 I watched a German plane drop a stick of bombs on nearby oil tanks. The fire was to last three weeks and claim the lives of five Cardiff firemen.

We went on our flat-backed lorry to dig slit trenches in which the firemen might shelter from machine-gunning planes. When we left Pembroke for the quiet of Pontypridd, the fires were still burning.

Harry Hartill
PONTYPRIDD, GLAMORGAN

On to something that will forever stay in my mind. This was the blitz on Manchester and Salford. On this particular night we were on patrol on the moors above Greenfield and around ten o'clock the sirens went and we heard the familiar drone of German planes approaching in what seemed like never-ending numbers. Soon afterwards the bombs started to fall in huge

numbers on Manchester and Salford, only 12 miles distant from where we stood helplessly watching as bomb after bomb was unleashed on the defenceless people of these two cities.

The sad memory of that night always comes flooding back to me on Armistice Day when I hear those familiar words, 'At the going down of the sun and in the morning we will remember them.'

Frank Buckley
OLDHAM, LANCASHIRE

It was all very serious. One of my scout friends had his hand smashed by an incendiary bomb hitting it, and I believe he lost two fingers. Another rode straight into

From left to right: Dennis Brooks, 'Chem' Chamberlain after having his hand smashed by an incendiary bomb, Jack Shardlow (Scout Troop Leader), wounded in Italy

a bomb hole on his bike. He was only bruised, and I remember at the time we all thought it was quite funny. It wasn't so funny later because when he was old enough he became an RAF navigator and was killed over Germany. My brother was wounded in both arms in Ceylon when he was in the Navy, and three of our Rover Scouts were killed later in the war and our Troop Leader wounded in Italy. I also lost a good pal in Italy. He was in the paratroops and was only 19 when he was killed. Such a waste of wonderful people.

Dennis H. Brooks
BURTON JOYCE, NOTTINGHAM

PART X

Going on to the Regular Forces

'Going ashore that evening we came across large numbers of the local Home Guard. They were doing a very efficient anti-invasion exercise, and for the next few hours I suffered the most devastating homesickness I have ever known.'

ALBERT JOHN FREEMAN,
MABLETHORPE, LINCOLNSHIRE

I enjoyed every minute of the Home Guard, but at the age of 18 I joined the Regular Force of the Fleet Air Arm.

My particular memory of that is that when I joined up Portsmouth docks had been bombed, and all the clothing stores had been destroyed. It was three months before I got a full uniform. There was me thinking I would get a new pair of shoes right away when I joined up, but I was soon disillusioned. I had left home with a pair of old shoes with holes in the soles, and I stuck it out as long as I could and then I sent an SOS out to the Old Lady, 'Please send me a pair of shoes, Mam.' I wonder how the youth of today would react to that.

Robert A. Eland
SCARBOROUGH, YORKSHIRE

I joined the Royal Navy in October of 1941 and the Home Guards all told me that they were very sorry that I had to go. I must say that the Home Guard stood me in good stead because in the Navy I became something of an expert gunner. I would not let my brother-in-law 'knock' the Home Guards because for all the jokes about them they did finish up doing a very good job.

Bill Thomson
SEATON, ABERDEEN

I am quite certain that Home Guard training served me very well, because when I joined the real army I was far ahead of those who had not been members in knowledge of arms and discipline. It might have been a joke at times but there's no

doubt the volunteers were genuine in their desire to defend their land.

Roy Elmer
WINDSOR, BERKSHIRE

From the time that Great Britain declared war on Germany in 1939, Bradford became a boom city. Mill chimneys that hadn't belched smoke for years started belching again with all the fury of pent up idleness. The British Army needed khaki uniforms. The mill workers of Bradford knew how to produce them.

Young men in their thousands were being called to The Colours. 'Bloody marvellous,' I thought. Everybody's off to the war and there's me stuck here in a cloth factory working for ten bob a week. At 15 years of age I told my sister Kathleen one Saturday morning how disgruntled I was with my boring job, and I was going off to the war. 'You're far too young,' she replied sweetly, knowing that it was only the brashness of youth talking. Kathleen was seldom wrong, but nevertheless with my usual pig-headedness I went against her advice. It was to cost me a day's wage and a new pair of shoes.

At the time I was getting on towards 16, and knocking around with a mate who went under the name of 'Winchester'. It wasn't his proper name, but he had a bad habit of repeating himself when in speech, and that's how it came to be. He also had a bad habit of talking people into doing things against their better judgement, and I was always one of them. 'Now then me mate,' he twittered, sidling up to me in a crablike approach one Sunday evening while I was kicking my shins with nothing to do. 'I hear you want to get into the war.'

'Course I do,' I replied wondering if he'd found some method. 'Why?'

'Well I'm off to join the Navy tomorrow, fancy coming with me?'

'Well,' I said slowly hesitating a few moments and wondering in my mind's eye if bell-bottom trousers would suit me.

'Well, d'yer fancy coming with me or what?' he repeated, living up to his name.

'What about our ages?' I asked. 'You're only 15 the same as me.'

'It's a doddle,' he chirped, 'it's a doddle. All you have to say is that we're both 18. I had a mate join and he was under age same as us.'

'No kidding?' I replied.

'No kidding, Scull,' he replied. 'No kidding at all,' he said with a cocky grin. 'We'll blob work tomorrow, then set off to Leeds.'

'Leeds,' I exclaimed sharply. 'Why Leeds?'

'Cause that's where the Recruiting officer is for the Royal Navy, dumb bell. You can't join the Navy in Bradford,' he added with a silly smirk.

'I didn't know they had dockyards in Leeds,' I said sarcastically, wiping the silly smirk from his face. Nevertheless with a clasp of the hand the pact was sealed.

'Be at the bottom of Leeds Road at ten o'clock, ten o'clock sharp,' he repeated, sidling out of sight.

'How much bloody further?' I asked Winchester aggressively as we clambered to the top of Thornbury roundabout on our way to Leeds the following morning. The clot hadn't told me that he'd no bus fare, and that meant a nine-mile journey still to go before we hit the Recruiting Office. Finally we tottered up the stairs of the Royal Navy Recruiting Office, to be thwarted at the door by an NCO of the Royal Marines who seemed to be as tall as a sailing ship and twice as breezy.

'We've come to join the Navy,' piped up Winchester who was on about a level with the buckle of the marine's white belt.

'You've come to join the Navy?' repeated the tall marine doing a 'Winchester'. The voice came in a harsh rasp somewhere about four feet above our heads. 'How old are you, sonny boy?'

'Eighteen, Admiral,' replied Winchester cheekily, sensing that already all was doomed.

Just as cheekily back came the reply. 'Call again when you've grown some fuzz around yer balls the pair of you, and we'll see what can be done.' With that, 'white belt' threw us a curt nod of dismissal. 'And douse those bloody cigarettes. They'll stunt your growth,' was his parting shot as we clattered down the stairs.

The following year, 1940, between switching jobs and switching girlfriends, my family was breaking up before my very eyes. My eldest sister Rosie had a poorly husband who had recently been invalided out of the army after serving with the BEF in the retreat to Dunkirk. Kitty, the next eldest, had a husband freezing to death somewhere in Iceland with the Duke of Wellington's Regiment. Next to go was Jimmy, who although he was a skilled mechanic, ended up unwillingly in an infantry mob with the Yorks and Lancs Regiment. The only people remaining were Aunt Nellie and Uncle Tommy who were both still working busily and 'coining it in', as they say in Bradford. Like the long-lost son they ushered me into their comfy abode whenever I appeared in my Home Guard uniform on their doorstep.

'I always knew you'd make it, lad,' said Uncle Tommy in a steady voice as though I'd just escaped from Dartmoor.

By this time the Americans were at war with the Japanese and not to be outdone Germany and Italy declared war on the USA, which reciprocated. Apparently everybody was getting in on the act, and there was I still farting around playing silly buggers in the Home Guard.

By now I was filling out fast and approaching manhood, and so 'know all' Uncle Tommy thought it about time that a growing lad like me was introduced to his personal compound at 'The Sun' Working Men's Club.

Germany is ready to collapse. That was Uncle Tommy's reasoning when discussing the war situation with me whilst drinking my first ever pint of beer. I nodded wisely in agreement. Why not? He had paid for the beer I was drinking and besides I was 'bull-shitted' up to the eyelids in my new Home Guard battledress, and my West Yorkshire cap badge shone like a beacon in the club's smoky atmosphere. I felt that all eyes were upon me. I bathed in the warm glow.

'Thar can take my word for it, lad,' he spouted with

all the confidence of an armchair general addressing his troops before going into battle.

In May 1942 at the age of 18 I joined the queue of young men forming outside the Mechanics Institute inside of which was the Army Recruiting Office.

'You're a silly little bugger,' said my sister Rosie with a catch in her voice. 'Those Germans are bigger than you.'

Two hours after joining the queue I was celebrating my admission to His Majesty's Armed Forces in one of the town centre pubs.

'What regiment have they put you in?' asked a spotty-faced youth who had failed his medical.

'The Bedfordshire and Hertfordshire,' I replied with a touch of pride in my voice.

'Never heard of them,' he said with a touch of jealousy in his.

Funnily enough neither had I. Not that I was going to give him the satisfaction of my not knowing.

'It's reckoned to be a bloody good regiment,' I countered giving him a baleful stare.

'Bullshit. They'll tell thee owt, as long as they get thee in,' he said sourly, lifting up his pint.

Finally, 'The Sun' Working Men's Club, Bradford. Near closing time. It was the last night of my embarkation leave.

'Nay lad, 'twill be a waste of time sending thee. T'war will be over by time thar gets in there. Get thee sen a pint, make mine a bitter, and get thee Aunt Nellie a bottle of stout.'

'Uncle Tommy knows best,' I said to myself, marching up to the bar.

Bill Scully
BRADFORD, WEST YORKSHIRE

I had to join the army proper when I was 18, and although we were told to forget all we had been told in the Home Guard, I did know a bit by then about rifles, Bren guns, grenades, gas masks, etc. I found this quite useful, but I did get caught by that old army trick. 'Does anyone know anything about...' This time it was 'Does anyone know anything about music?'

I stepped forward as I had learned a bit of violin at school and of course I then found out what it really meant. We had to carry the piano from the NAAFI to the Sergeants' Mess with the help of the other idiots who had given the wrong answer as well. Motto – never volunteer.

Reginald Underwood
IPSWICH, SUFFOLK

I n 1944, after being a Naval Gunner in convoys for a year and seeing the war at first hand, my ship docked at Middlesbrough, and going ashore that evening we came across large numbers of the local Home Guard. They were doing a very efficient anti-invasion exercise, and for the next few hours I suffered the most devastating homesickness I have ever known.

Albert John Freeman
MABLETHORPE, LINCOLNSHIRE

[E]ventually] I was told I was no longer in a reserved occupation and had to report to the Regular Army.

After six weeks' primary Infantry training I was asked if I wanted to join a Regular Rocket Battery. I replied that I was a tradesman and so had a trade test and went straight into the Royal Electrical and Mechanical Engineers.

Three and a half years later I finished as a sergeant, in India.

Eric Wall
LETCHWORTH, HERTFORDSHIRE

When war was declared on Sunday 3 September 1939 I was 16 and a half years old and was employed as a milk roundsman by Lowestoft Co-operative Society Dairy, delivering milk to customers in the Beaconsfield Road area of South Lowestoft. Just before 11 o'clock on that Sunday morning, one of my customers invited me in to listen to the Prime Minister,

Neville Chamberlain, broadcast to the nation on radio stating that as he had received no reply from the German Chancellor by 11 o'clock we, Great Britain, were now at war with Germany. Little did I realise that two and a half years later in February 1942, I would be called up for military service in the army and to be known as 6924136 Rifleman Horn, K., the Rifle Brigade and it would be five years later, in 1947 at the age of 24, before I would be a civilian again.

Kenneth Horn
LOWESTOFT, SUFFOLK

I was 16 when I joined the Home Guard. On my eighteenth birthday I volunteered for air-crew duties in the RAF. This was the only way farmworkers could get into the forces in 1941. After a wait of over six months my days as a private in the Sussex Home Guard finally came to an end. However, my time in the Home Guard, together with subsequent service in the Royal Air Force, qualified me for the Defence Medal, and I recall obtaining a certificate of my Home Guard service when applying for my campaign medals at the end of World War Two.

Bob McGill
WEST HADDON, NORTHAMPTONSHIRE

Without pushing myself forward in any way, I was promoted to lance corporal [in the Home Guard] but in my heart I knew that I would never make a good soldier. I doubt whether I ever hit an inner, or even the target with either a rifle or a Tommy gun bullet. I was not mentally or physically equipped for fighting and disembowelling a straw dummy with a bayonet disgusted me.

Peter Cane Vigor
LUTON, BEDFORDSHIRE

PART XI

Standing Down

'We, the AA Home Guard, who were alone engaged in actual combat on a regular basis against the enemy, were accorded the honour of the rear position of thousands taking part in giving and taking a salute from their King and Queen and the Princesses and a great multitude of the British population.'

LEN BARTON, WINGHAM, KENT

When the threat of invasion was removed in June 1944, things got a little more relaxed and everyone was just coasting along, knowing that it was just a matter of time before it was all over and we could start picking up the threads of normal life again. During the last 12 months of the war, the despatch riders were given much more freedom to arrange their own training exercises, so we usually went out into the country and did some grass track racing or hill climbing up some of the Clent Hills with disastrous results to some machinery if one was too ambitious. This could put one out of action for some time as spares were non-existent for the ancient machines being used.

Eric Gregory
TAMWORTH, STAFFORDSHIRE

Although the Home Guard, which had become a powerful well-equipped force and had stood guard at Buckingham Palace, wasn't disbanded until 1944, my involvement came to an end somewhat earlier. The physical problems that had caused the Medical Board to reject me at Dover Street when called up eventually made it very difficult for me to carry on, and my own doctor said 'Enough' and gave me a letter to present to Captain Purser. As a result I had to have a further examination but that confirmed my own doctor's opinion, and so I returned to the drill hall where I was instructed to hand in all my equipment.

Having done this I was in civvy street again. Since the end of the war German military archives have revealed conclusively that there was a huge relief in German High Command circles when I left the Home Guard, but by that time the invasion of Britain was out of the question.

John Slawson
HEYWOOD, LANCASHIRE

I continued my service career until the Home Guard 'stand down' and participated in the March Past in London, in which we, the AA Home Guard, who were alone engaged in actual combat on a regular basis against the enemy, were accorded the honour of the rear position of thousands taking part in giving and taking a salute from their King and Queen and the Princesses and a great

multitude of the British population. We also enjoyed the concert given that evening in the Albert Hall, London, appreciating the appearances and services of so many of the radio and music hall stars of the day. We, of 24Z, had also had our own local 'stand down' parade around several miles of the West Ham neighbourhood that same morning.

Len Barton
WINGHAM, KENT

S ome time in 1945, and certainly before VE Day, we of the Home Guard were disbanded.

But before that happened we did a series of Victory Parades in which all the units in Leicestershire gathered together and paraded through the streets, and I remember that the very last parade of all was through the streets of Hinckley.

The one disappointment I have of those years is that I wasn't allowed to claim a Defence Medal as all the others in the unit did. I was told not to apply as I had joined the Home Guard under age, and did not qualify, being so young. At this time I was still so young that my mind didn't dwell on such things as medals. But as I have grown older I can see the injustice of the system as I did all that the others did and faced what others faced in the way of risks and danger.

Albert Squires
BLACKPOOL, LANCASHIRE

As the war neared its end a parade was organised to take place in Palmer Park in the east end of Reading. On a very hot Sunday we marched from Yeomanry House through the town to the Park where we joined up with the other companies and, with an audience of Reading residents, paraded and did a march past to the colonel in chief. We then marched back to HQ. Thankfully we had a good brass band playing us along which made it a lot less tiring.

Soon after this the government decided that the Home Guard would not now be needed and after a social evening at HQ at which we were allowed to bring wives and girl friends, we were disbanded.

Cyril Bird
FRIMLEY, SURREY

At last 'our war' in the Home Guard was over. Rifles were cleaned for the last time and returned, our bits and pieces and Sten guns laid aside. Peace had returned to the country and it was certainly quieter at weekends. Each member received a certificate from the government at the time and a very nice thank you letter.

Arthur Fairhurst
BURY, LANCASHIRE

The last year of the Home Guard my mate and I volunteered to go on the guard at the sub station. I don't mind admitting that we were both sweet on two of the Women's Air Force people. But as usual we got the last guard which was 4–6 a.m. It was snowing and freezing like hell and after an hour my mate said to me 'let's go in' which we did.

The corporal in charge was like the one in *Dad's Army*, so we took no notice of him. We were young men of 21 years. We took our boots off and lay on our beds but after a few minutes the door was flung open and there was the duty officer, Captain 'somebody or other', and his lieutenant bellowing, 'Where's the guard?'

We were told we would be reported to army headquarters at Chester and charged.

Later at work we were told it had in fact all been reported to Chester and we would stand trial. Being only 21 we worried for a week or more and then suddenly the Home Guard was stood down. What a relief. But I have often wondered now I am older how I could be 'tried' for not carrying out a job I had volunteered for in the first place.

Leslie Owen Allen
CREWE, CHESHIRE

After the war, Home Guards were presented with medals and ribbons (brown in colour for bullshit) but I threw mine away; I had earned no medals and the reasons I joined were not because I believed that war settled arguments or hatred of Germans, but because

I wanted to show some sense of loyalty to my country and if I had to take part in what I considered silliness, I would rather do it in the fresh air as far as possible, and avoid Civil Defence and First Aid training in the Nissen huts behind the canteen (ill-ventilated and blacked out). Our company took part with the other services in a Victory Parade through the main street of Luton. I tried to spruce my uniform up and appear soldierly.

My wife, Mary, and my sons were spectators lining the route and although they waved flags and cheered with the rest, they laughed at my appearance and Mary said I marched like a weary ploughman crossing a ploughed field. And she was right.

Peter Cane Vigor
LUTON, BEDFORDSHIRE

PART XII

Final Reflections

'[It] says a lot for the people of this island that when Anthony Eden asked for volunteers, they came forward in their hundreds of thousands, old and young, fit and unfit, with a spirit I don't think we shall ever see again.'

JOSEPH O'KEEFE, DUNSTON, GATESHEAD

The worst didn't happen. Whether Hitler ever intended to launch an invasion of this country we probably will never know. Happily, for us that is, the German hordes were thrown against the Soviet Union and from that moment Germany lost the war, though much horror and suffering had to be endured before the end came. But if this country had been invaded and if enemy forces had fought their way up the country and were poised to sweep up to Lancashire and towards Heywood in particular, then I'm sure that the lads of the 20th Heywood would have put up a stout defence. We would have fought them on the bowling greens, having first got the permission of Charley Cain the Green Keeper to do so. We would have fought on the allotments, assisted no doubt by Mr and Mrs Grindrod who would have defended their plot at Pot Hall to the last stick of rhubarb.

John Slawson
HEYWOOD, LANCASHIRE

I cannot praise too highly the conduct of the civvy services, and the public at large. The bravery and fortitude of all those people brought home to me at least the realisation that we were all in the war together, and even today if ever I hear anyone passing unqualified remarks about what a person did in the war I have no hesitation in setting that person right. In fact in many, many ways the people who had to stay home and provide the fighting forces with means of combating the

Axis showed equally courageous conduct.

An outstanding example was of course the Home Guard consisting as it did of the boys who were too young, and the older men, who for one reason or another were not acceptable to the Forces at the time and paraded with unqualified 'weapons' to train with I might say determination, not to mention great enthusiasm.

The services of these men did not go unnoticed and neither did the young women who went into the factories and the NAAFI canteens to bake the everlasting rock cakes and other off duty snacks for the troops billeted in and around Ascot. I sometimes think that the mainstay of the training troops was beans on toast.

Jim Dyer
NORTH ASCOT, BERKSHIRE

Looking back on this time in my life I have just realised I spent almost ten years at war. What with joining the Home Guard and then being called up for Army Service and fighting in Palestine until I was demobbed in 1949, it took half my childhood and all of my teenage years, and the overriding memory I have of that time is one of hunger. The shortage of food haunted me. Even in the army after the war they did not give much food. All my army pay seemed to be spent buying food from the NAAFI.

Albert Squires
BLACKPOOL, LANCASHIRE

I was always glad that I had served in the Home Guard. It gave me a good basic training for when I was 'called up' in early 1942. At least I wasn't thrown in at the deep end like some of the others. I had already learned to drill, handle and fire a rifle, throw hand grenades, and I didn't have to learn from scratch from the army instructors who, as I recall it, had forgotten the art of civilised conversation when they got frustrated with us. Many a mother would never have recognised her instructor son at such times.

If some people found us amusing I wonder if they realised we were of the same material as the partisans of Russia, Poland, France, etc. They did not find them amusing. The civilian soldiers in those countries were a pain in the neck for the Germans, and I am sure we would have been just the same if we had been invaded. It is possible that if Hitler had invaded, the cream of the Home Guard, the young and fit, would have been taken into the army or formed into a huge guerilla force to hold down a large section of the German army.

My memories of the Home Guard only cover the period of the start of the LDV till early in 1942, when I was called up in the Royal Artillery, but they were happy days. Like many other people we never thought we could lose the war. Maybe our youth and enthusiasm blinded us to the massive forces that could have been thrown against us, but it says a lot for the people of this island that when Anthony Eden asked for volunteers, they came forward in their hundreds of thousands, old and young, fit and unfit, with a spirit I don't think we shall ever see again in this country. Everyone united and determined to try and stop anyone daring to invade this island.

Joseph O'Keefe,
DUNSTON, GATESHEAD

Looking back I wonder if we would have done any good at stopping the Germans if they had invaded. We might have delayed them a little but we only had ten rounds each, so if parachutes had come down whilst on Hob Hill, we could only have shot a few, as we had no telephone or radio to warn anyone else.

We would only have put up a token resistance. I left in 1941 to join the Royal Engineers and saw service in the Middle East and Italy, ending the war by spending three years in hospital. The training I had in the Home Guard was helpful to me in the army but the Engineers was a different thing altogether.

John H. Scoby
REDCAR, CLEVELAND

Our war effort finally died of inertia. We gave in our rifles and bayonets, ammunition, the old Vickers machine gun and my Browning Automatic. While Rusty heaved the ponderous Blacker Bombard to its final resting place.

The Bank House Club, our headquarters for the duration, rang no more to the nightly roll call and the banter.

Most of us enjoyed our days in the Home Guard but how we would have fared in battle is another matter altogether. However, my theory is that given good equipment and expert training, we would not have let anyone down.

Tommy Wilkinson
ASHINGTON, NORTHUMBERLAND

Most of us had friends in the thick of the fighting and some of us had lost some very good pals. It's difficult to say what the outcome would have been had an enemy force landed but I'm sure with our knowledge of the local countryside we should have played an important part in delaying any enemy forces that had managed to land. However, we never had to put into practice the skills we had learned.

As the news from all battle fronts began to improve, the Home Guard was disbanded in September 1944. Farewell parades were held, all weapons and equipment were handed in and we all went our separate ways. Looking back I enjoyed every minute of it.

Wilfred Hodgson
CONINGSBY, LINCOLN

Acknowledgements

We received a huge amount of support and help on the first publication of this book from the individuals who have written their stories.

So we have pleasure in recording our thanks to:

All the former Home Guards who have so willingly told us of that very special period in their lives and the lives of their families.

All those others who were not in the Home Guard but were present at that time and have recorded their memories.

Roy Rowberry of the Leamington Spa Branch of the Home Guard Association for the valuable information he gave to us.

Again also we must not forget Jane Stew, Shirley Cartwright, Judy Crawshaw and Margaret Young who did all the typing so we could 'put it all together'.

Thank you all very much.

Frank and Joan Shaw

Index

Entries in *italics* indicate photographs.

Index of Contributors

Entries in *italics* indicate photographs.